40p

MESSENGERS OF
GOOD
NEWS

DEREK TIDBALL

Scripture Union
130 City Road, London EC1V 2NJ

© 1989 Derek Tidball

First published 1989 by Scripture Union
130 City Road, London EC1V 2NJ.

Designed by Sue Ainley
ISBN 0 86201 483 2

Scripture quotations in this publication are from the Holy
Bible, New International Version. Copyright © 1973, 1978,
1984 International Bible Society. Published by Hodder and
Stoughton.

British Library Cataloguing in Publication Data

Tidball, Derek
  Messengers of Good News
  1. Bible. Characters
  I. Title
  220.9′2

ISBN 0–86201–483–2

Phototypeset by Input Typesetting Ltd, London

Printed and bound by Cox & Wyman Ltd., Reading

Contents

Dedicated to
Gilbert W Kirby
in appreciation

Preface

Preachers always *say* that the great giants of the Bible were people just like us, but were they *really?* As I have mulled over these twenty characters I have been surprised to find how very real and believable they are. No two of them are alike; their personalities and characters are all different.

What is more, they will not conform to any nice 'Christian' strait-jacket we may try to impose upon them. In fact, we would probably allow only a few of them into our churches today, and hardly any into our pulpits because they would not conform to our expectations of what a spokesperson for God should be. Some are certainly gentle and gracious but others are argumentative, radical or embarrassingly unconventional.

I have also been surprised by the sheer variety of the methods God uses to convey his message. Sometimes it is through a quiet whisper, a gentle hint in a private conversation; sometimes he speaks through the thunderclap of a prophet who denounces a whole civilisation. He speaks through visions, poetry, drama, academic argument, history, straight preaching, song and story and even through silence. It is all here. We lose a lot by treating God's colourful mosaic of communication as if it were a dull monochrome.

The most striking fact to emerge from seeing these characters in action it that God uses us, through his grace, *warts and all*. Often it is actually our weaknesses and the individual emphases of our particular character that he delights in most, using them especially to achieve his own ends.

I have not always stayed with the 'big names' in the Bible. Some of the characters here are given only the briefest of mentions in the Bible but they were God's messengers all the same. You will find here a mixture of public and private messengers, vocal and silent ones, men and women. I hope you will be able to find *yourself* too, somewhere in these pages and be given the confidence, if you do not already have it, to let God speak to others through you.

I have dedicated this book to Gilbert Kirby, who has been a friend since I became his student eighteen years ago. He has often been a wise counsellor to me as well as being a great encouragement to my ministry, as he has been to countless others down the years. The year in which I write sees the fiftieth anniversary of his ordination. I, with many others, am grateful for this messenger of God.

1

Moses

Facing up to limitations

Conversations can get going in the strangest of places. I first began to speak seriously with Enid in a funeral car as we were driving the twelve miles from the church to the local crematorium to say the final farewell to her father-in-law. Until then we had had very little contact but afterwards she started coming to church, was converted and became one of the most effective gossipers of the gospel we had. But you would never have thought that possible if you had been in the car with me that day.

Enid was a 'charlady'. She had had twins when she was forty, which was a bit of a shock to her as well as to everybody else, and she had been under the doctor 'for her nerves' ever since. Her older boys were a worry to her. Even her delightful husband had gone through a rough patch with his nerves a few years before and needed a lot of support. Although Enid had grown up in the Sunday School she had forgotten most of what she had been taught. That was obvious the day she came to a family service in which there was a drama about Jonah and she asked me, as she left, where we had got hold of such a good yarn. She had no idea it was in the Bible.

She was very conscious of her own inadequacies and limitations and if we had ever asked her to do anything publicly she would certainly have said, 'No! I couldn't possibly . . .' Yet soon after her conversion she was sitting down with her friends, and with families in some of the neediest parts of town, doing Bible studies with them. What an evangelist she became in spite of all her disadvantages! Doors were open to her where the rest of us would never have been welcome.

It would not have occurred to her to think that she had anything in common with Moses. Yet he too was a messenger very conscious of his own limitations.

Moses was a shepherd in the back of beyond. As he clocked on to tend his sheep one day, I doubt if he thought anything special was about to happen. But what took place at the 'burning bush', as we call it (for the simple reason that it did not burn!) was to turn his life upside-down.

'Now Moses was tending the flock of Jethro his father-in-law, the priest of Midian, and he led the flock to the far side of the desert and came to Horeb, the mountain of God. There the angel of the Lord appeared to him in flames of fire from within a bush. Moses saw that though the bush was on fire it did not burn up. So Moses thought, "I will go over and see this strange sight – why the bush does not burn up."

When the Lord saw that he had gone over to look, God called to him from within the bush, "Moses, Moses!"

And Moses said, "Here I am."

"Do not come any closer," God said. "Take off your sandals, for the place where you are standing is holy ground." ' (Exodus 3:1–5)

Who? Me?

Exodus chapters 3 and 4 tell us about the meeting Moses had, there in the desert, with God. It was probably the most crucial meeting of his life but he had no advanced warning of it. Moses found that God had already set the agenda and by the time he realized what was happening, God was well into the first item on it. There was no time to prepare his case, no time to think up ways of diverting God's attention to other matters. God confronted Moses 'in the raw'. So we find out what Moses was really made of.

He did not let God get further than item one on the agenda: a proposal that Moses should change his job to that of shop steward for the Israelite slaves in Egypt. Basically, the job was simply that of speaking out for God but Moses came up with five convincing reasons for why he was not suitable. His reservations are ones we have all felt, if not actually spoken, when confronted with the same challenge.

Objection one: '*I am a nobody*'

'I am sending you to Pharaoh to bring my people the Israelites out of Egypt' (Exodus 3:10). Moses' initial reaction to this plan, like David Wilkerson's when called to work among the drug gangs of New York, was one of shock. 'Who am I, that I should go to Pharaoh and bring the Israelites out of Egypt?'

How interesting! All his early life he had been a Some-body, the adopted son of Pharaoh's daughter. Now he sheltered behind the excuse that he was a nobody. During his first forty years he had tried to use his position to improve the lot of the Israelites in Egypt. But that had led to disaster; he murdered an Egyptian and had to run for his life. For years now he had been nothing but a runaway prince with a price on his head; an unknown herdsman, living in obscurity. What good could *he* do?

God must have welcomed Moses' feeling of inadequacy. The school through which he had put him for the last forty years had obviously done its work. He was no longer full of himself and his own plans and was now in a position to be used by God.

So God has a ready answer to his objection: 'I will be with you.' It is God's presence with his messengers which makes all the difference. In the end it is not our eloquence, knowledge, brilliance or gifts that matter, but simply whether God is with us or not.

We need to handle our feelings of inadequacy carefully. If those feelings are genuine, they can help us rely more on God. Often, however, such feelings are self-induced; we think it is spiritual to feel that way and we do not want to fall into the trap of pride. Or we can overplay our feelings of inadequacy simply to get out of doing the job. Either of these responses to a task which needs to be done is crippling to the church. Both of them stand us in need of God's forgiveness.

Like most pastors I frequently approach people to take on a responsibility in the church. The reply is often, 'No, I wouldn't be any good at it.' The reasons given for this rejection are usually quite untrue (and cast grave doubts on my judgement as a pastor!). Moreover, it means that the same few willing work-horses have to shoulder yet more of the burdens and certainly more than is good for them. I am sure the response arises from a genuine sense of inadequacy, but it is one which could be overcome.

Pride is a sin but so is false humility. It often prevents us from serving Christ when we could do so very adequately. The Bible teaches that every believer is gifted in some way (1 Corinthians 12:7; 1 Peter 4:10); so why do we say that we do not have any gifts? What is more, false humility casts doubt on the integrity of God. If he has said he will be with us why are we so afraid?

The feeling that we have nothing to offer is a major cause of the church's ineffectiveness in reaching others for Christ. God's word to us today is the same as his reply to Moses. Jesus called us all to a new job when he said, 'Go and make disciples of all nations.' And he added, 'I will be with you always, to the very end of the age' (Matthew 28:19–20).

Objection number one seems to have have been answered.

Objection two: 'I do not know enough'

Moses is not so easily convinced. Thinking quickly he tells God that he does not have enough experience of him to do the job. He does not understand the issues properly and does not have a good enough grasp of theology. 'Suppose I go to the Israelites and say to them, "The God of your fathers has sent me to you," and they ask me, "What is his name?" Then what shall I tell them?'

We have all played the 'just suppose' game. 'Just suppose I witness to Justin and he asks me about the Trinity, what could I say?' 'Just suppose I talk with Jane and she asks me about the problem of suffering, how do I answer?' 'Just suppose I talk with Martin and discover he's a Jehovah's Witness; I won't know what to say.' 'Just suppose I talk to my mates at school and they tell me that Christianity is rubbish because it's been proved that God was an astronaut.' Just suppose . . . just suppose . . . And because we are so busy supposing, we say nothing. We are frightened into silence by our own imagination.

Moses is certainly not going to be excused so easily. God's answer this time is to reveal himself to Moses in a remarkable way – perhaps the most remarkable way in the Old Testament. 'God said to Moses, "I am who I am. This is what you are to say to the Israelites: 'I AM has sent you.' " '

There is a wealth of meaning within these few words. This revelation of the divine name is both profound and simple. It speaks of his existence: he is, he lives. It speaks of his nature: he is the source of all being, the ultimate and self-existent life. All other life is dependent on him. *We* have to say, 'I am, because . . .' Only God can say, 'I am.' It says something about his sovereignty and power: it might equally be translated, 'I will be what I will be.' He freely determines the future and shapes the destiny of creation. It says much about his mysteriousness: when we have said the most profound things about God we have not even begun to understand him.

God then pointed out to Moses that this should not really have been news to him. He is the God of the patriarchs and Moses would have known of their faith and tradition. Perhaps the more significant thing for Moses was that he had now met this God for himself. God was no longer someone he had heard about second-hand. Now that Moses had met him personally he would forget about presenting him to other people as a 'set of ideas' or so many cold facts.

This encounter with God perhaps explains why Moses became so certain and dogmatic about God. He had met him first-hand and could speak about him with conviction. No matter how good our theology is, people will only be convinced by our witness to Christ if they see that we have met him for ourselves. Our first task as Christians is to witness to the living Christ, not to try to explain the Trinity!

I remember being at an ecumenical conference on theology when one high-ranking participant was pouring scorn on the idea of being born again. Then, a Yorkshire housewife who had no theological training spoke up in her broad accent of the way she had been born anew and the changes it had made to her life. The cleric confessed that it made him think again; he could not dismiss evangelical theology so glibly when it was expressed with such kitchen-sink authenticity.

Objection number two has been answered.

Objection three: '*I am afraid of failure*'

It is at this point that God moves on to item two on the agenda, Moses' detailed job description (Exodus 3:16–22). He is told what he is to say and do. He is also told how people will react and how God will deal with them.

But still Moses objects. 'What if they do not believe me or listen to me and say, "The Lord did not appear to you"?' He is afraid that he will find himself in a minority of one, with no way of proving that God has sent him. He will make a fool of himself and end up a laughing stock. Couldn't God do something to guarantee that he would be taken seriously? Fear of failure can always make us clam up when we feel we should speak out for God.

Actually, it is probably the last thing Moses should have worried about for when people really meet with God, as Moses had, others know it. It silences people's quibbles.

Again, God stops to give Moses the reassurance he needs. God asks him to take part in a miraculous transformation of three ordinary things. At God's command, Moses throws down a stick and it becomes a snake. He picks it up and it turns back into a stick. God commands him to put his hand in his coat and take it out. To his horror Moses finds he has developed leprosy. God tells him to put his hand back in again and he is healed. Then, on the strength of these two miracles, God promises that the Nile will flow with blood instead of water when Moses is in Egypt to present his message to the Israelites. His part in these miracles will only be to pour out onto the ground a bowlful of the river water.

The answer to the fear of failure is simple: do not underestimate the power of God. But we will not experience that power until we step out in faith and use the ordinary things God has given us. If we fail to throw down the stick, or to put our hand inside our coat, or to pour out the water on the ground, we will not see the miracle. So whatever the ordinary thing is that God has given us - words to speak, neighbours to care for, people to love, homes to use for hospitality – until we use them we will not see God transforming them.

Objection four: 'I have not got the gifts'

Moses now complains specifically that he is not gifted in the right way for the job of spokesperson. He is not 'eloquent'. He never had 'the gift of the gab' and it does not look as if God is going to give it to him now. Would it not be better for God to recall his selection panel and consider someone else who had been short-listed for the job?

Moses was right in one respect. An encounter with God does not necessarily give us every gift or solve all our problems. It may sort out many things, but will often leave others which have to be worked through over a period of time at a quite ordinary level. Many people who have received specific ministry feel very let down when, later, they still have to battle through their problems or face the consequences of their past sinful way of life. But what *has* happened is that their encounter with God has changed them, making them able to cope with those problems in a different way even though their circumstances remain the same.

Moses did not realise that God never calls a person without equipping him or her to achieve the task. The will of God will never take us where the grace of God cannot keep us. It is on just this point that God now instructs Moses. 'Moses, are you really so ignorant? Do you really think that if I made you in the first place it is beyond my power to do a few simple adjustments here and there? I designed and created the mouth, so I can certainly make it eloquent when I want to.'

Objection number four has been answered.

Objection five: '*I do not want to go*'

At last the truth is out. Moses has run out of excuses and now tells God what he really thinks. He does not want to go. God's patience has been tested to the full. But even in his anger, God is gracious. He does not let Moses escape his commission but offers the companionship of his brother Aaron who can do the talking for him.

Moses has no option. Every objection has been satisfactorily answered. God has chosen his man and will use him. Now it is simply a matter of obedience. Moses needs to get started on the job.

How did Moses make out? What sort of a messenger did he prove to be?

A messenger with limitations

As the story unfolds we cannot help wondering whether it is a comedy or a tragedy. The sight is either very funny or quite pathetic. Two old men, in their eighties according to Exodus 7:7, one of whom is tongue-tied and neither of whom have any resources or plans, stand before the most powerful man in their world. They demand that he grants liberation to their people, who are an irreplaceable source of cheap labour as far as the despot is concerned.

Their initial attempts met with predictable failure and only served to make matters worse for the people they were trying to help. As a result, not even their own kith and kin were sure they wanted this intervention on their behalf.

But 'God chose the foolish things of the world to shame the wise' (1 Corinthians 1:27). His strategy with Moses was no exception. Incredibly, he said to this old man, 'I have made you like God to Pharaoh' (Exodus 7:1). Perhaps God was saying to Moses that he was going to catch Pharaoh in a trap of his own making. Egypt's religion was full of superstitious beliefs, one of them being that Pharaoh was divine. Yet he found that his divinity was being challenged by the God of the Hebrews: 'The Egyptians will know that I am the Lord.' What was more, all Egypt could see Pharaoh's 'divine powers' being challenged as the plagues swept the land. Even more galling for Pharaoh was that the challenge was thrown down by two vulnerable old men; their God apparently considered them to be a fair match for him.

Two facts become apparent from these early days of Moses' mission. Firstly, a call from God does not over-come all our limitations. Moses still suffered from them in plenty. But they were irrelevant to the success of his mission. In fact, his limitations may well have helped it. It was clear to Pharaoh that these two men standing before him had no power of their own, so someone greater than them really must be working through them.

That is often the way. I remember my surprise the first time I saw a man whose name I knew well as a first-rate evangelist. Could this crumpled cleric who looked anything but dynamic really be the man of whom I had heard so much? Like a king putting all his treasure in clay pots, God works through weak people 'to show that this all-surpassing power is from God and not from us' (2 Corinthians 4:7).

Secondly, our great aim still needs to be to let the world know that 'I am the Lord.' The secular world of our own day has little time for the living God. The vast majority of people never think about him seriously. They may allow him into their lives briefly in times of crisis, or they may develop a mixture of faith and superstition. But unless they are told about him they can have no real understanding of who God is and what he asks of them. Like Moses, who was not so very different from most of us, it is our task to bring people face to face with him.

Take it from here . . .

• God told Moses to speak to some specific people. Is there anyone particular to whom God might want you to speak about him: neighbours, family, people at work? Ask God to show you who he wants you to speak to.

• What excuses do you use to avoid talking to people about God? Spend some time listing those excuses and then bring them to God. Ask him to deal with the feelings that lie behind them; perhaps they are feelings of inadequacy or fear, or perhaps it is a lack of motivation.

• God helped Moses by giving him someone else to work with. Have you thought of asking a friend to pray with you, encourage you, give you confidence? If you think this would help ask God to help you find such a partner.

2

Caleb

Hanging in there!

I felt foolish! I was the padre of the summer missionary camp but I had lost my voice and was feeling asthmatic. What use was I to anyone? 'Don't worry,' my friends consoled me, 'Dr O'Hanlon will soon sort you out.' I did not like to tell them that others had been trying for years and failed but that is another story! It was only then that I noticed Lily O'Hanlon, a little woman who seemed quite old and who had a great sense of fun.

Only later did I realise how remarkable she was. Lily O'Hanlon was a missionary in northern India when, on 1 January 1933, God gave her the assurance that she would one day become a missionary to Nepal, the land of the hills and valleys of the Himalayas. It seemed impossible then since the land was closed to Christian missionaries. But for years Lily and others held on to the vision God had given until, in November 1952, the door opened and six missionary couples began the trek into Nepal. The Nepal Evangelistic Band (now known as the International Nepal Fellowship) was at last in action. For nineteen years Lily O'Hanlon had believed in the vision. After nineteen years of patient waiting and much praying, the vision became a reality.

Lily reminds me of Caleb. Neither character was

exceptional; they were just ordinary people with staying power. They are like thousands of others who have waited patiently for God to bring about the conversion of a loved-one or the fulfilment of a vision.

The nonconformist

Not long after the Israelites left Egypt they came to the borders of Canaan. The land God had promised them was already being lived in, so Moses wisely sent out twelve leading men, one from each tribe, on an intelligence-gathering mission. Caleb was one of the twelve, and the story is told in Numbers 13:1–33.

After six weeks they returned and the majority report was one of fear and caution. The land really was 'flowing with milk and honey' as God had promised, and they brought back some of the lush fruit to prove it. But . . . and it was a big but, 'But the people who live there are powerful and the cities are fortified and very large.' They felt that they could not recommend any advance, for this would mean certain defeat. The enemy was obviously enormously powerful, so the majority voted to stay in the wilderness. The crowd, gathered to hear the reports, went along with their verdict.

Then Caleb and Joshua entered a minority report. It was full of confidence: 'We should go up and take possession of the land, for we can certainly do it.' Caleb's bold intervention was meant to encourage the people not to be so feeble, but feelings were running high and the ten other explorers flatly denied that the land could be taken. The majority won and Caleb, with Joshua, Moses and Aaron, who were united in their desire to move forward, were almost stoned to death.

Why was Caleb so sure the land could be taken? He

might by nature have been an optimist and go-getter, but that was not why he urged the move forward. His motives were more soundly based. He had a *realistic* picture of the land he was sent to explore; he, too, had seen the giants and the walled cities and knew the size of the opposition they would encounter. He did not underestimate the difficulty of the task ahead. But as well as having a realistic picture of the land, he had a *God-given* picture of the land. The others had left their spiritual spectacles at home but he had taken his with him. So he saw the land through the eyes of a God who was greater than any enemies; a God who had given his promise that he would fight for them. The others had simply left God out of their calculations.

Without a vision the church soon dies, as is evident if you reflect on what has happened to the church in Britain this century. We have suffered from seeing too many of the obstacles and too little of the Lord. But the vision needs to have a sound basis, as did Caleb's. A vision which is merely someone's personal pipe-dream can set the church back as much as having no vision at all. A vision needs to be checked against God's revealed word and supported by proven spiritual leaders. If it passes these tests then the visionary must move ahead even if he or she finds few companions and years of patiently waiting before the vision is fulfilled. In the meantime he or she has to plan the way forward and deal with problems and obstacles to enable the vision to come true.

Everyone else cried, 'Back to Egypt!' Memories are short and the Israelites had already forgotten the hardship and oppression which they suffered and from which they had longed to be free. Not so Caleb. He was not backward-looking. He reached out towards the future and allowed himself to be controlled by the promise of

God. God said of him that he had 'a different spirit and follows me wholeheartedly' (Numbers 14:24). The others felt that God would not deliver on his promise. Getting them out of Egypt was one thing, but getting them into a land already well populated and heavily fortified was another. So God decreed that only Caleb and Joshua would enter the Promised Land. Those who had turned away from it, not believing that God wanted to give it to them, would never enter it. They would die before the fulfilment took place. Only Caleb and Joshua survived to see the promises of God fulfilled.

Before we react to God's verdict by saying that he seems to have judged the people harshly, perhaps even in a fit of temper, we should remember that he simply gave them what they asked for. They did not want to go to the Promised Land – and God would not force them in.

It is never easy being a nonconformist. But that is what the messengers of God are sometimes called to be. We do not have to be odd-bods or to deliberately provoke mobs in order to be ridiculed for our faith. Like Caleb we simply have to have a different spirit and follow the Lord wholeheartedly. If we do we shall soon find ourselves out of sorts with much of society and find the selfishness and indulgent materialism of our own day uncomfortable.

Rewarded at last

Caleb next appears in Joshua 14:6–15. There we discover that it took forty-five years for God to deliver on his promise. Caleb was forty when God promised him his inheritance of land and was eighty-five when he received it! Those intervening years had been desert years. Israel had just moved about in the desert, condemned by their own unbelief to a pointless existence. But Caleb did not give up or let his vision of God dim. He continued to believe that God would keep his promise and so waited patiently for that day.

The problem with us is that we want everything yesterday. Many of us would not have held out as long as Caleb, so we would have missed out on the inheritance. Although God may have given us a particular vision – perhaps for our family or the church – it may take years to come to fruition. There are battles to fight, obstacles to overcome and realities to be dealt with. The fable of the tortoise and the hare reminds us that it is often the plodders who get there in the end. Edison is said to have failed 3,000 times before he successfully made a filament for an electric light bulb! William Carey is quoted as saying, 'I can plod. That is my only genius. I can persevere in any definite pursuit. To this I owe everything.' 'Plodders for God' is an honourable club to which to belong! Caleb's patience was not passivity. Throughout the period of waiting he was alert and ready to take opportunities. When they came to him at the tender age of eighty-five, he seized them with all the enthusiasm of a teenager! Most of us would think we deserve a quiet retirement at that age. Not so Caleb.

When the land had been allocated to the Israelite tribes, Caleb had been given Hebron, a town which was situated nineteen miles south-west of Jerusalem. It was the highest town in Palestine – 3,040 feet above sea level. It was also the burial ground of the patriarchs and a town which Caleb himself had explored. But although it was 'his', Caleb still had to capture it! This was going to be no easy matter; it was populated by strong anti-Israelite forces. Caleb could have gone for a softer option. But at eighty-five he enthused to Joshua, 'Now give me this hill country that the Lord promised me that day. You yourself heard then that the Anakites were there and their cities were large and fortified, but, the Lord helping me, I will drive them out just as he said' (Joshua 14:12).

Eighty-five and still fighting for God! Still growing in God! Still keen for God! Caleb reminds us that however old we are we still have hill country and enemy territory to conquer.

There is a great place for the gifts and experience of the elderly in the church. It is dangerous to retire spiritually when we have retired occupationally! Retiring from a job, or having more time on our hands when the children leave home, may in fact release us for Christian service and herald the arrival of our most effective years for Christ. Those who are retired are ideally equipped to do so much, especially visiting, listening and caring, as well as administration and maintenance. There is even the possibility of going overseas to serve Christ as a number of recently retired people have done. If you are retired, in what ways are you using your gifts? Or as a church, in what ways are you making the most of the gifts of your elderly members?

Caleb certainly did not attribute his remarkable stamina to any qualities of his own. His only explanation was that he had wholeheartedly followed the Lord. Whatever our condition or situation what matters is that we do the same.

J Oswald Sanders has written of Caleb: 'In youth he stood alone, in mid-life he walked alone, in old-age he climbed alone.' There is a loneliness about being a great survivor. True messengers of God will often find themselves in the same situation.

Take it from here . . .

- Has God given you a vision – someone who is going to come to know him, or a new area where work for God could be carried out? Can you help make that vision a reality? Here are some ideas for how to get things moving: share the vision with others; pray for the person or situation; ask God to show you any steps you should take.

- Perhaps you do not have a vision of your own (yet!). Then do you know anyone who has? How can you get involved with their vision – perhaps by praying, supporting, being ready to plod alongside them? Note down any Christian organisation you know of which has a new vision for God's work and think of ways you could support them. If you are not aware of your church's vision for service and evangelism ask your church leader about it and ask how you can help towards making that vision become a reality.

- Have you planned your retirement? The advertisers tell us it is never too early! Take some time now to think about how you could use the years ahead for God. Do not be afraid to dream dreams: what would you *love* to be doing for the Lord in ten, twenty, thirty years' time?

3

Deborah

Tuning in to God

Can God use a woman? Many people in the church have their doubts. Over the years I have seen many gifted women graduate from Bible College and go on to become members of local churches where their gifts are unrecognised and wasted. They are well qualified and, were they men, they would immediately be asked to lead a house group or stand for the PCC or the diaconate. But they are women. I can think of at least two Christian societies which have been happy to have women holding the fort during an interregnum but would not have appointed them to a permanent position of leadership. Of course, it is different on the mission field, where women can do everything! But at home . . . !

Down the centuries the attitude has been the same. Although God has frequently raised up women preachers or prophets, more often the concern of church authorities has been to suppress them. George Fox, the founder of the Quakers, deserves credit for insisting on the right of women to be involved in leadership. But many Quaker women who were brave enough to take such a step suffered for it. Dewens Morrey was whipped for preaching in 1657 and Mary Dyer hung for it in 1660. Today we are more civilised in our reactions but we still have problems in using the gifts that God has given if he has given them to a woman. Perhaps Deborah can help us.

After the conquest of Canaan under the military command of Joshua, the history of Israel became depressing. For centuries the people condemned themselves to a perpetual cycle of disobedience to God, which brought his punishment, followed by their searching for God again and his deliverance of them through the work of a judge. God must have asked many times, 'When will they ever learn?'

Can God use a woman?

As we read the book of Judges we are just settling into a repeat of the cycle when we are rudely interrupted (Judges 4 and 5). The judge with whom we are confronted is a woman, Deborah – and a married woman at that. As the story unfolds it becomes more incredible. For *twenty years* Deborah was the nation's *chief judicial officer*. She operated down south. But there was trouble up north, where the people were being oppressed by a ruthless foreign soldier called Sisera. The Israelite tribes in the north were not, however, able to sort things out themselves. Deborah, who was living much further to the south had to take the initiative if anything was to be done about the situation. With amazement we read that she appointed an army commander from the north, but that he refused to fight unless she was there to give support. She therefore went into battle having become not only the nation's chief judicial officer but also the *commander in chief of her armed forces*. Victory followed but only after another woman, Jael, had the courage to assassinate Sisera. The honour again goes to a woman. Deborah then led the nation *in worship* and composed a song of praise which is full of both strength and beauty.

Some people are amazed that a woman is to be found in this position because they have learned to read the Bible wearing the spectacles of male chauvinists. They might speak of her as 'the best man in Israel', for instance, as some speak of Mrs Thatcher as 'the best man in the Cabinet'. This itself is derogatory of women in its holding up of men as if they were the measure of all things. Several commentators go in for special pleading and try to establish the case that Deborah is only allowed to occupy such an honoured and leading position because the men have failed to accept their God-given reponsibilities and roles within society. But there is no hint of this in the text. It seems to speak naturally of a woman as leader and shows not a whiff of embarrassment that this should be so. God is often not so restrained in whom he uses as we think he should be!

The people God uses are not always from the social category we expect. Deborah may have been a woman but God used her in leadership as he has thousands of others, before and since. Men might tend to discount women in leadership roles but God does not. The history of the church at home and abroad is filled with women, without whom battles would never have been fought and victories would never have been won.

There are also other categories of people that we tend to assume God cannot use in leadership: those who come from a social class that is different from our own, for instance. Again and again we see God defying our expectations. Often it is those people who have been rejected by the church authorities or missionary selection panels that are the very people God has chosen to use.

Tuning in to God

Deborah is first of all introduced as a prophet. Miriam (Exodus 15:20) was given the title before her. Huldah (2 Kings 22:14) is to follow in her footsteps. In the New Testament Anna (Luke 2:36) and the daughters of Philip (Acts 21:9) are also recognised as prophets. And these are only the ones who are named.

What is a prophet? In Deborah's case the crucial factor seems to be that God revealed information to her about future events and present situations. Deborah's command to Barak to engage in battle with Sisera came not from her but from the Lord (4:6). She was confident in her prediction of victory, not because she had calculated the military strength of the opposing armies but because the Lord had given his word (4:14). She even knew what would happen to Sisera because the Lord had revealed it to her (4:9).

Deborah's most outstanding quality was not, in fact, her ability to lead but her ability to stay finely in tune with God. Her sensitivity to God was seen in her judgement of individuals and the prediction of the battle, and also in her instinctive reaction after the battle. She immediately turned the victory celebrations into a praise meeting not into an orgy of self-congratulation. She did not neglect God when success came her way but straight away exalted him in his sovereignty and righteousness. To speak God's words at the right time and in the right way we need to be closely in touch with God at every step. My own experience of working with a number of women in Christian leadership suggests that this sensitivity may be a special contribution that they can make, but by no means the only one! I thank God for several women who wisely have stopped men blundering in because they were in tune both with the heart of God and the feelings of people.

Sharing God's concerns

It is possible to see Deborah, and even more Jael (4:17–22), as if they were vicious and blood-thirsty women. How can such women be held up as examples of messengers of God? And what sort of God is it that they represent?

Our tolerant age is uncomfortable with the picture of the warrior God presented here. But should it be? We need to realise that Israel is struggling for her very survival. Either she defeats her enemy or she goes under. Our problem often stems from the fact that we have too much sympathy for the enemy! They were hardly the nice, polite diplomats we imagine them to be, who would have loved to live in peaceful co-existence with Israel. They were vicious and unsparing in their cruelty. They would not have spared a second thought as they raped and pillaged and trampled all over the people of Israel. They were evil. And if good is to survive, evil must be eradicated.

It was not Deborah's concern to be vindictive. She did not rejoice because Israel had got her own back. She rejoiced that justice had been done. These were the enemies of the *Lord* (5:31), as was clear from the way they treated the Lord's people and the Lord's moral laws. The justice and righteousness of God was at stake.

Deborah shows us that there is a real place in God's service for people with moral fibre. We are engaged in spiritual warfare and must be concerned to work for the defeat of evil in all its guises. The way we do so today will be different from the way it was done in Deborah's day. There is no licence here for crusading armies or for witch-hunts. Times change. But in appropriate ways, through our democratic system and involvement in the nitty-gritty of politics and public affairs, whether it be in the form of the local parent-teacher association or by standing for Parliament, we need to fight the moral and spiritual battles of our day. God give us more Deborahs!

Take it from here . . .

- What does your church expect from the women in the fellowship – a responsible use of gifts and talents or just an endless supply of tea? It is easy for women in some churches to lack confidence because for so long nobody has expected (or allowed) them to participate to any great extent. If you are a woman, what can you do to gain the confidence and the opportunities to use and develop the gifts God has given you? If you are a man, what can you do to encourage the women in your fellowship to use their gifts more fully?

- 'Deborah's most outstanding quality was not, in fact, her leadership ability but her ability to stay finely in tune with God.' It can take time to develop sensitivity to God's voice; how are you developing your sensitivity to it?

- 'We need to fight the moral and spiritual battles of our day . . .' What local issues do you think you should get involved in, in order to fight for a more just, compassionate and spiritually healthy society? How will you go about doing this?

4

An unnamed servant
Being a link

Halfway through a week's evangelistic mission in our church I was struck by how 'improbable' was our choice of missioners. I am sure they will understand what I mean. We had invited Marilyn Baker, the well known gospel singer, and her team. What is improbable about that, you may ask, when Marilyn's track record as a recording artist made success a foregone conclusion? Well, Marilyn has been blind since her early childhood and one of her team members, on whom she greatly depends, is deaf! Tracey suffered from encephalitis when very young and had a hard childhood to cope with as well. Marilyn serves as Tracey's ears while Tracey serves as Marilyn's eyes. Together they give a powerful testimony to the grace of God in situations which we would normally regard as tragic. Their effectiveness lies in their ability to speak very naturally about the way God has shown his grace to them in their disabilities. They were not always evangelists. For some years before becoming a full-time singer for God Marilyn was a school teacher. They are just ordinary people who are experiencing the grace of God in their darkness.

God can bring good out of tragedies if we will let him. I know a great many people who have suffered some major mishap like a serious road accident, or some grief like the loss of a child, or some sadness like the break-up of their family. Yet they have not only maintained their faith in God but been open to him to use them through it. And he has. Others have become bitter, resentful and closed their lives to God, not wanting anything more to do with him. Sadly, he has been unable to use them to bless other people and, just as sadly, he has been unable to pour his love into their own lives.

There was a young girl in Israel who knew how to handle tragedy so that it could become a blessing. She had nothing much more than a walk-on part but it was enough to set off a train of events which almost brought two countries to war. The story is told in 2 Kings 5:2–3.

A personal tragedy

Relations between Syria and Israel were rarely smooth. Even during their quieter moments, when outright fighting died down, cross-border raids continued. On one of these raids the Syrian soldiers captured a little Israelite girl. Separated from her family and from all that was familiar to her, her future was very uncertain. Imagine the fear and loneliness she must have felt as she was placed in the slave market in Damascus waiting to be bought as if she were some cheap animal. Would she become the plaything of some cruel master who would sport with her and then discard her or would God be merciful and would she end in the home of a kindly master? God was in charge, even in the darkest of moments. Matthew Henry can even speak of the young girl being 'providentially carried captive to Syria', for it was through her calamity that God was going to bring mercy to Naaman and his family. It was to his household that the little Israelite captive was taken.

Naaman was a soldier and a good one at that. King Ben-Hadad had said all sorts of nice things about him and heaped many honours on him because he was a military genius. But his future career was blighted by a fatal flaw. He had leprosy. It was probably not of the worst kind, the sort we think of today, since Naaman was not made to live in quarantine. Even so, his skin disease was an embarrassment of the highest order and he was urgently in need of a cure.

No one seemed to know quite how to respond when the little unnamed servant girl stepped onto the stage:

'She said to her mistress, "If only my master would see the prophet who is in Samaria! He would cure him of his leprosy." '

Her brief words tell us three things about her.

Concerned love

She was concerned about her master's health and welfare. She could have taken the attitude, as some Christians seem keen on doing, that his suffering was the judgement of God on his life or, simply, that it 'served him right'. He was, after all, a pagan and had inflicted much suffering on her country. She could have simply shut her eyes to the need and pretended that it was none of her business. But she did not. Her words were prompted by a concerned love.

She was true to the faith in which she grew up and knew that God's love is never channelled through narrow confines whether of nationalism or of our own selfish desires for revenge. She would have been taught that he was a God whose love included 'the stranger and the sojourner'.

This girl was a pioneer in cross-cultural evangelism and refused to let the racial divide stand in her way. In divided Britain today few of us follow in her footsteps. We are content to keep within our ethnic groups, and even *encourage* churches to have an ethnic bias, rather than make the effort to bridge the man-made divides which Christ came to abolish (Ephesians 2:14–18). We may never express our racial prejudice explicitly. We more often do so subtly, simply by avoiding those with a different skin colour or by refusing to offer them the same hospitality as we would those of a similar background to our own.

This can never be an authentic expression of the gospel.

Responding to need

Secondly, the servant girl may not have known much but she knew enough. She knew that there was a prophet in Israel who could help. She did not have the gift of healing herself and may not have been able to answer all the questions she might have been asked. Did she ever realise, I wonder, that although Elisha had worked several miracles, he had not yet healed any lepers (Luke 4:27)? Did she even know that his name was Elisha? Never mind, she knew enough to point Naaman in the right direction, and that is often all God requires of us.

Persistent faith

Thirdly, she trusted God. 2 Kings 5:3 records her bold

words: '. . . the prophet . . . would cure him of his leprosy.' Should she not have hedged her bets a bit more? What would happen if she were proved wrong? She had faith in the power of the living God and knew that he would prove himself.

Faith is an indispensible ingredient for all those who want to see God at work. The role of faith in bringing about miraculous healing is evident throughout the Gospels, especially in Mark's. For long stretches of time in the church's history, a lack of faith meant that few miracles took place; we never looked for them or asked for them. Today, perhaps we are in danger of letting the pendulum swing too far in the opposite direction. 'Claiming' something from God and then putting him on the spot to produce the goods is not necessarily an act of faith at all. Nor is it right to make bold claims about what God is going to do, and then blame the church or the individual concerned for a lack of faith when those claims are not fulfilled.

God does not work miracles and healings for our personal convenience but for his glory. True faith is not our own wishful thinking but our response to God's word to us. So when we 'claim' something from God, are we genuinely responding to what God has revealed to us about that situation or merely trying to force God's (or the church's) hand in the matter? Let's have faith but let it be a genuine confidence in God and in his revealed will.

The girl spoke out just at the right moment: Naaman was desperate and willing to listen: 'Naaman went to his master and told him what the girl from Israel had said.' People who would not normally take any notice of the Christian faith are often open to it in moments of crisis. It was the right moment in another sense too, because Israel and Syria, usually at daggers drawn, were enjoying

35

a rare time of peace. So the way was open for Naaman to visit Israel and be healed. ' "By all means, go," the king of Aram replied. "I will send a letter to the king of Israel." '

We have often thought with a wry smile of the pomposity which Naaman showed as he made the mistake of going, all trumpets blazing, on a diplomatic mission to the king of Israel, instead of going quietly to a humble prophet. We have often listened to the way God had to humble him through Elisha's command to dip himself seven times in the dirty river Jordan in order to be healed. We have been amazed at the power of God to heal him and the love of God to do it to someone who had often opposed him and his people. But have we thought of the little girl who was the catalyst? Her two sentences made it all possible.

Take it from here . . .

- Have you had any dark circumstances in your own life? Think of one now. Take time to bring it to God and ask him to use it for his purposes.

- Think of someone you know from another religion. What is it that 'makes them tick' or is of real importance to them? You may need to do some research on their beliefs . . .

- Think of one or two non-Christian people you know who, like Naaman, are facing insurmountable problems. How can you bring God's help and support to them?

5

Jonah

Writing in the written-off

Have you ever attended a Shakespeare play done in contemporary costume? Watching *A Midsummer Night's Dream* where Bottom and his friends are dressed as Hell's Angels is an interesting experience and it does bring home, with fresh impact, the meaning of the play!

A modern Jonah

If we were to tell the story of Jonah in contemporary dress it might go something like this.

God told a member of the Free Presbyterian Church in Northern Ireland to go and preach in Dublin because he had observed how wicked the city was. You would think that the preacher would have welcomed his assignment, despite the risk of being attacked by supporters of the Irish Republican Army (IRA). After all, what could be more satisfying than to go into enemy territory and preach hell fire and damnation?

Unpredictably, however, the preacher cannot face the thought of going there to preach to them, and decides to get away from it all. So he makes his way to Larne and catches the night boat to Stranraer. Stranraer lies on the mainland, in the opposite direction altogether from Dublin. He would be out of God's sight there.

That night a storm brews and the ferry is tossed about like a cork in a jacuzzi. Before long the ship begins to roll over and the preacher is thrown overboard without any hope of being rescued. Somehow, though, he is miraculously rescued and thrown up on the shores of his native Ireland. God graciously asks him a second time to go to Dublin and this time he obeys.

He makes his way into the city but does not really know where to begin. He has little option but to start shouting at street corners and in market places, tactics hardly likely to produce any positive results except to get him thrown out quickly. But a remarkable thing happens. People stop and listen. They start responding to what he says. The media pick up the story and he appears on the evening's news. He is given an interview with the Prime Minister of the Republic who accepts what he says and publicly encourages people to repent. A great revival breaks out all over Dublin as people turn to God. Support for terrorism and corruption of all forms ceases and the political tensions of north and south are eased as never before this century.

And what happens to the star of the show? Where is the preacher? Well, he is sulking, in hiding on the outskirts of the town. At last we get to the truth of the matter. He had never wanted to go and preach in Dublin, not because he was afraid, but because he felt so strongly that those people deserved judgement. He had more than a sneaking suspicion that God was going to do the dirty on him: Dublin would repent and God would let them off the hook.

Up north, the preacher would never be able to look his friends in the face again. He would be a laughing stock. The Dubliners deserved the worst that judgement could give them for their support of the indiscriminate acts of cruelty of the IRA. The last thing any of the preacher's friends would welcome was a change of heart and reconciliation. They would not believe the southern repentance was genuine anyway, nor accept the southerners as brothers and sisters in the Lord. No wonder the preacher felt betrayed by God, lonely and miserable, even suicidal.

The original story

This modern parallel is not intended to encourage anti-Catholic bigotry! The message of Jonah should do quite the reverse. It knocks the pride of those who think they are spiritually superior. The parallel does, however, give us an inkling of the emotions Jonah would have felt. Not all the details of the original story of Jonah have been included in the modern parallel. We did not mention, for example, that he was rescued by a big fish who then proceeded to disgorge him on the sea shore. But so many hours have been spent discussing whether this could be possible that most of us have failed to grasp what the message of the book of Jonah is all about. It is not there to stretch our credulity about big fish, so what is the message?

The point is that Jonah was prejudiced about God's grace. Generally he was pleased to share the fact that God longed to forgive people for their wrongdoing and to restore his relationship of love with them. But there were limits. Jonah could see why God might be gracious to people like himself. But outside the limits were people like the Ninevites – they were known for their cruelty and they simply did not deserve God's grace.

It is not until the end of the book that Jonah reveals his hand. 'O Lord,' he grumbles, 'is this not what I said when I was still at home? That is why I was so quick to flee to Tarshish. I knew that you are a gracious and compassionate God, slow to anger and abounding in love, a God who relents from sending calamity' (4:2). And Jonah did not like that. He would have preferred a God who gave people what they deserved. He did not like the idea of a God of unlimited grace. It was outrageous. The wrong people would get into heaven that way! Heaven should be for the good, or at least for the not very bad, the kind, the respectable and the religious; not the violent, the cruel and the riff-raff!

The book of Jonah is not simply the story of one man and his struggle with the profligate grace of God. It is also a parable about its original readers and about us today. There is a bit of Jonah in us all. The book would originally have been read or listened to by religiously observant Jews in the kingdom of Judah. They would have been shocked that God had called Jonah, a man from the religiously lax kingdom of Israel, to be a prophet. They would also have been shocked by God's choice of Jonah because he had been an advisor to Jeroboam II, king of Israel, and had presumably supported his corrupt regime (2 Kings 14:25). God should really have been much more careful about whom he used. On top of all this, God sent Jonah to Nineveh, to people who were not Jews and whose reputation for wickedness and cruelty was infamous. God's love and grace were proving to be too extravagant for the comfort of his people.

God challenged Jonah to break out of the rut into which he had settled. He was channelling the grace of God only to people like himself and was surprised to discover the compassion of our missionary God who goes out to find those who have turned their backs on him.

Modern-day Ninevehs

In recent days there have been powerful demonstrations of the extravagant grace of God in the prisons of Northern Ireland. Members of modern-day Ninevehs have been turning to God because others in the province have learned to go where God sent them. Charles Colson in his recent book, *Kingdoms in Conflict*, tells a little of the story. He writes of Gladys Blackburn, a retired school teacher less than five feet tall, who went on Christmas Eve in 1980 to visit prisoners. She was directed to Chips McCurry, a former member of the Ulster Volunteer Force (UVF), convicted of murder. He heard Gladys Blackburn say that he needed to accept Christ as his Lord, just like the thief on the cross; and he did. The years of hatred which had been with him since he was twelve years old, when his father was murdered by the IRA, then rolled away. Today Chips McCurry is entering the Baptist ministry.

Just as remarkable is the story of Liam McCloskey and Jimmy Gibson. Liam McCloskey was an ardent member of the Irish National Liberation Army (INLA), a Marxist offshoot of the IRA, and one of those who almost died in a hunger strike ordered by IRA authorities in the Maze Prison. His near-death through that strike brought him to his senses and caused him to give his life wholly to God. Recently he appeared on a platform with Jimmy Gibson, a former loyalist paramilitary in prison for attempted murder, who had also come to Christ. McCloskey commented that once, 'if I had seen Jimmy on the street, I would have shot him. Now he's my brother in Christ, I would die for him.'

This is where the true hope lies for Northern Ireland and for every cruel and tortured part of our world. It is realised when ordinary men and women overcome the Jonah syndrome and take the love of Jesus to those eaten up with hatred.

We sometimes sing:

> 'There's a wideness in God's mercy,
> Like the wideness of the sea;
> There's a kindness in his justice,
> Which is more than liberty.'

But do we believe it? The outrage of God's grace means that he loves the men in the white South African police force, the IRA terrorist, the fanatical Islamic hijacker, the fugitive Nazi war criminal. Closer to home, it means he loves the Birmingham punk, the 'social security sponger' in West Ham, the unmarried mother and the addict. And that is uncomfortable.

Take it from here . . .

- Take some time to think about the depths of God's love and forgiveness towards you. Remember that you did nothing to earn it, but that God gave it to you freely through Jesus. Praise and worship him.

- Now make a list of the people you know whom you cannot imagine responding to Jesus. Thank God that his grace is just as freely available to them as it is to you! Start praying that the Holy Spirit will help them to respond to Jesus' love.

- What new ways could you use to communicate the gospel to those people on your list? Ask God to help you know what to say and how to say it.

6

Hosea

Speaking from hurt

The question is being raised more frequently today: can God use a person in Christian service whose marriage has broken down and whose family life is fractured? A growing number of ministers are finding that they are no longer wanted, for this reason. It is the policy of some missionary societies not to employ divorcees, and some parachurch organisations are equally reticent, claiming as their justification Paul's teaching in 1 Timothy 3:1–13 about the high standards required of elders and deacons.

It is not only full-time Christian workers who face this problem. Many Christians with ordinary jobs, in love with the Lord and with a deep desire to be useful to him, have faced the pain of a family split. Afterwards, they often feel too ashamed to continue the work they were previously doing in the church and feel that they have failed their Lord. They believe themselves to be an embarrassment to him and so withdraw. So they add to their existing pain the further burden of isolation. Frequently the church encourages them in this course of action.

Is it right that we should adopt this stern approach? The Bible makes clear that much is expected of those who would serve Christ and it seems uncompromising in its teaching that divorce is wrong (Malachi 2:16; Matthew 19:3–12). In a society where marriage seems to have been greatly devalued there is an obligation on the part of the church to uphold biblical values. But does this mean that such people are written off by God and ruled out from serving him further? The life of Hosea says, very emphatically, 'No.'

Having agreed on the need to teach biblical truth on marriage and family life, we must also recognise that there is more which must be said. Our God is the God who uses the Hoseas of this world.

When Hosea came onto the scene it would have looked, to the casual observer, as if the northern kingdom of Israel and the southern kingdom of Judah were both enjoying a period of peace and prosperity. The truth however was a little different. The sins which Amos had condemned had continued unabated and the children of God were worshipping any god but Yahweh. They were proving unfaithful to him in their worship and by their conduct. In addition, there was a growing threat from the neighbouring state of Assyria which was increasing in power and hostility. The warning bells were beginning to sound for the people of God.

A living example

God deliberately sent Hosea to address their situation. Hosea's unhappy marriage became the means by which God spoke to his people about his love for them. We know little of Hosea before he became a prophet except that he came from the northern kingdom of Israel and was the son of a man called Beeri. It has been suggested that Hosea might have been a baker as his prophecies used illustrations which seem connected with that trade.

When Hosea responded to God's call to become a prophet to the people, he gave God the right to use every aspect of his life to get the message across. But I doubt that Hosea was ready for what God asked of him. No sooner had the call come than he was told to, 'take to yourself an adulterous wife and children of unfaithfulness, because the land is guilty of the vilest adultery in departing from the Lord' (1:2). It was a scandalous request. Was God really sure about what he was asking of the prophet? It seems almost offensive that a man of God should be asked to marry a prostitute, or at least one who, if she was not already a prostitute, was going to become one.

Why did God subject Hosea to such indignity and humiliation? Simply because he could not have made his point more powerfully than by portraying it in the life of one of his servants. 'The Lord said to me, "Go, show your love to your wife again . . . Love her as the Lord loves the Israelites, though they turn to other gods . . ." ' (3:1). God also chose this method because it moulded Hosea and gave him the ability to speak more feelingly about God's love than anyone else had ever done. His message was forged on the anvil of painful personal experience. His imitation of God's searching and unrequited love was very powerful.

Gomer was certainly to make life far from easy for Hosea. She gave birth to three children and all were given names which signified the nearness of God's judgement. The first, a son, was called Jezreel (1:4), the name of a town where a former king had conducted a bloodbath. God had not forgotten this act and had decreed that punishment would soon come to those involved. The second child, a daughter, was called Lo-Ruhamah, meaning 'not pitied', 'for I will no longer show love to the house of Israel' (1:6). She was a warning that God's patience was running out. With the third child the prophecy of God's coming punishment reached its climax. He was a son called Lo-Ammi, that is, 'not my people', 'for you are not my people, and I am not your God' (1:9). Unless something drastic happened to cause a change in his people, God would soon write them off.

As the mother of these three children whose names bore such vivid warnings from God, Gomer might have been expected to take the threats seriously. Instead she ignored God's instructions about faithfulness in marriage and committed adultery. It would appear that having left Hosea, she ended up in slavery. What was Hosea to do? Forget he ever knew her? Blame her, as everyone else did? Or go on loving her?

God commanded Hosea to go on loving her. So he set off to buy her freedom and bring her back home. Then he took steps to restore their relationship (3:2–3). His action was an acted parable of the love of God. The people of Israel had committed spiritual adultery by ignoring the true God and worshipping false gods. Yet God wanted to go beyond 'being reasonable' in forgiving and restoring his people. He was committed to healing their waywardness and loving them freely (14:4). Here was love that could be rejected and abused and yet remain firm.

God's choice and use of Hosea is telling. If God can deliberately use the devastating experiences of one of his prophets to proclaim the depth of his own love, then he is more than able to use others who have also been through such harrowing times.

This is not to say that we should be careless about mistakes in the past, or about family tensions or splits in the present. They are serious and they matter. But they do not disqualify us from being used by God. It is worth noting that Hosea was the 'innocent party' in this matrimonial dispute. So today, there are often those who are more sinned against than sinners in cases of divorce, even if our present law with its 'no guilty party' stance might suggest otherwise. Many who have found themselves in that situation have developed a special sensitivity to others who are vulnerable and have been fashioned by their own painful experiences to be invaluable messengers of God.

Forgiveness and restoration

Even where a person was the 'guilty party' and responsible for initiating the breakdown, God can forgive, restore and recommission. The fault needs to be freely admitted and confessed. Patterns of behaviour which led to the unfaithfulness need to be changed, with professional help if necessary. We need to face up to our continuing weaknesses and take preventative action to ensure that there are no repeat performances of the past. But having said that, the God of the Bible is a God of new beginnings and of restorations. He seems quite happy about using ex-murderers, like Moses, ex-adulterers, like David, ex-betrayers, like Peter and ex-bigots, like Paul. That surely gives all of us hope that we can be used by God in the future.

It is when we are most vulnerable and at the end of our own resources that we are of most use to God (see 2 Corinthians 12:9). Rob Frost is a Methodist minister who wrote recently in his book *Breaking Bread*,

'As I look back on my preaching ministry I sense that God has used me most effectively in three situations: when I've been scared, when I've been sick and when

I've been shattered. In other words, when I've reached the end of my own resources and cast myself upon the Lord.'

Exactly. You do not have to be perfect or in perfect condition to be a messenger for God.

Charles Colson, the former adviser to President Nixon who was sent to prison because of his involvement with the Watergate scandal, now leads a hugely influential prison ministry. In his book, *Loving God*, he writes, 'My greatest humiliation – being sent to prison – was the beginning of God's greatest use of my life. He chose the one experience in which I could not glory for His glory.'

Take it from here . . .

- God's dealings with Hosea remind us that we are called to love and forgive again and again. If you are involved in a situation or relationship where there is a need for God's love and forgiveness, how will you convey that message by word or actions?

- Do you know any families that are going through a bad time? Is there any practical way in which you can support them? Maybe you could help by looking after the children, or being a listening ear?

- How willing are you to let God use your experiences to help others? If you have been through painful experiences yourself, have you been able to accept – and feel – God's forgiveness, healing and restoration? If you do not feel that you have, or if you are going through a bad time at present, talk to your pastor about it.

7

Joel

Challenging the superficial

Some people never seem happier than when they are pronouncing the doom of the world. Whether it be AIDS, some natural disaster or financial collapse, they rub their hands with delight and say, 'It's judgement! This is from the Lord! It serves you right!' Such people seem to believe that God is, in C S Lewis's words, a 'cosmic sadist'.

Most people in our unbelieving world react to these interpretations with scepticism and amusement. If they do not take God seriously, why should they be bothered by warnings about his judgement? They understand natural disasters in terms of purely scientific explanation.

Yet, if we are to be true to what the Bible teaches about God we must believe that he is capable of exercising discipline and sending warnings through natural disasters and tragedies. As creator he is still intimately involved in the running of the world and that means not only that he usually makes the place run smoothly for our benefit but also that occasionally he is equally able to tug the reins and give us a jolt when he feels it to be necessary. The problem lies in finding a way to say that to a secular world so as to be heard and understood. The man who walks down Oxford Street with a placard saying 'The end is nigh' simply does not provoke the right sort of reaction. If you feel that you can see God's judgement working out in natural events, take a look at Joel, who felt similarly, and see how he handled this perception.

We know little about Joel. His name was a common one meaning, 'Yahweh is God'. This may well be significant in the light of his task, which was to speak to a generation who did not believe that Yahweh was God, and could not have cared less anyway.

We cannot even be sure when Joel preached but it was certainly after God's people had returned from exile. Before the exile prophets were critics of God's people but afterwards the emphasis of their message changed. They became the comforters of a struggling community who were in danger of being sucked under by problems on every hand. In such circumstances it was hard to maintain a vital and active faith in God, and many did not.

Joel was goaded into speaking by the onset of a plague of locusts. We know from contemporary descriptions that such a plague can be one of the most frightening experiences to live through and it can have devastating effects on agriculture and, consequently, the economy. With evocative poetry (1:2–12, 2:1–11) Joel described the locust invasion they had experienced and then explained why it had taken place. It was, he said, an 'army' sent by the Lord and led personally by him as a warning that a final day of judgement was coming. 'The day of the Lord is great, it is dreadful. Who can endure it?' (2:11). The people's sin was provoking God's anger and God was giving them a chance to take stock and change. Joel must have been a brave man to come out with such a statement. It is never popular to attribute natural disasters to God. How did he get away with it?

Uncovering fears

On the surface, people may seem to believe that life is safe and sure, but underneath we know that routine life is very fragile. Storms, plagues, disasters or war can soon shake our confidence and cause immense anxiety. Joel recognised that and tried to interpret his nation's fears for them. But he always did so in such a way as to lead them out of their fear to find a right security in God. He did not gloat over their misfortune but balanced his emphasis on judgement by an emphasis on God's grace. 'Return to the Lord your God, for he is gracious and compassionate, slow to anger and abounding in love, and he relents from sending calamity' (2:13).

Joel knew how to capture people's interest. What he said connected with the experience of the hearers and his words must have seemed like windows through which they could see a wider picture. In the context of the bigger picture their own experience made sense. The sheer forcefulness of his descriptions combined with the skilful imagery he used made Joel's message compelling. Having started from the real concerns of the people, he managed to keep the people with him as he developed his case. What he had to say to them would have been as unwelcome as a scientist explaining to a meeting of undertakers that he had just discovered the secret of eternal youth.

The whole of Joel's prophecy was directed towards the future. He stressed that what they experienced today was a herald announcing the imminent arrival of the future. In a way, the future had already begun.

It is hard to get people to see that. The young person is not put off smoking because he is told he will die of lung cancer in thirty years' time. Nor does the drug addict come off cocaine because of the threat of what might happen to him in the future. Neither can imagine it happens *to them*. Even so it would be irresponsible not to warn and help, and Joel did so with a great sense of urgency. He stated clearly that those who would not listen to God's warnings and continued to live unrighteous lives would face God's judgement in the future when he put an end to all that is evil (3:1–16).

Giving hope

But Joel was even more concerned to give hope and to assure people that there is no 'iron law' of determinism at work making judgement inescapable. He longed for the people to return to God, for those who did would find the future would take a very different turn. It would bring in a time of rich blessings, poured out by the Spirit of the Lord. His people would experience God's complete salvation (2:28–32, 3:17–21).

People who are 'up against it' need hope, not negative condemnation. The hope we offer them must be well-grounded, not the sort of wishful thinking that assures the terminally ill patient that she will soon be recovered and at home again. It needs to be a hope which is founded on the character of God.

It is the sort of hope held by people in the persecuted church. I shall never forget a Christian couple who lived in Eastern Europe. By our standards they had little. Some days during the winter they had no gas or electricity except briefly in the small hours of the morning. Food was scarce. Added to the troubles they shared with everyone in their country was the fact that they were Christians and were regularly harassed for their faith. 'How on earth do you survive?' we asked them, amazed not only at their fortitude but their cheerfulness. 'Ah,' they said, 'we are the people of the future.' They knew, as Joel did, that one day unjust regimes will be brought to nothing and that those who have faith in God will be vindicated.

It is not easy to be a contemporary Joel, burdened by the sin in the world and crushed under the conviction of coming judgement - judgement which seems so real as to be already at work. It is easy to let such a burden degenerate into mere judgementalism and to distance ourselves from those we condemn rather than going to them with a heart of compassion that woos them into responding to the grace of God.

Few people are effective 'Joels'. If you desire to be one then mix your unapologetic message of warning with tears and blend it with a message of grace. Look hard at what words and images you are going to use so that you can convey your message with skill. And where there is a response do not depress your hearers further but give them hope.

Take it from here . . .

- Check today's newspaper. Do you think there are any events which may be a sign of God's judgement? Try to 'get into the shoes' of those people with whom you can least easily identify. Pray for those people; bring them before God and ask him to change them.

- Check your skill as a communicator. How could you explain your response to the daily paper to a friend who is not a Christian?

- Check yourself! How are you allowing the future to change your present?

8

Zechariah

Seeing with God's eyes

When I applied to join the ministry I was visited by my area superintendent. If his objective was to put me off, he was very nearly successful. He spent an hour depressing me with the news that we were increasingly a denomination of smaller churches, that there really was not very much hope for us in the future and, in any case, we had too many ministers. The decade of the sixties, from which we were just emerging, was certainly a very disheartening decade for those in Christian leadership. The church was in decline and it had suffered from seismic social shifts which had pushed it firmly to the margins of society. Many faithful servants of God were a bit battle-weary and their vision for the future was at a low ebb.

At the same time, others were receiving a new vision from God which gave them a sense of confidence and purpose for the future. Eventually that vision was caught by large numbers in the church with the result that the church is in much better shape now than it was twenty years ago.

Vision is important. As Proverbs 29:18 puts it in the famous Authorised Version, 'Where there is no vision the people perish.' We know it from recent history, too. John F Kennedy's and Martin Luther King's effectiveness in mobilising and motivating their generation lay in their ability to set before them a dream of a just and different society. We know it from our own recent church experience. Where ordinary members of the church have no vision then God is limited in what he can do through them. But once, after communion with God, they regain their vision and believe that God is still powerful and able to work, even if the work he is going to do will be a little different from what he did in the past, then he can work again.

Zechariah was a man of vision at a time when God's people were inward-looking and lacking in vision. He was probably among those who returned to Jerusalem after the exile with Zerubbabel and Jeshua (see Nehemiah 12:4). He was from a priestly family and so had a particular burden for the future of the temple.

The situation in Jerusalem was far from easy. It was difficult to make a living and the struggle for sheer survival was uppermost in everyone's mind. Nehemiah and Ezra had begun to rebuild the city and with it, the heart of the nation. But nothing was achieved overnight. For some time the temple lay in ruins. The people had other priorities than putting hard-earned money or much-needed labour into rebuilding the house of God. And even when they did think about doing so the depressives among them got to work to extinguish any flickering incentives they might have had. The new temple, they said, wouldn't be a patch on the old. It couldn't be. It would be a small and poor successor to the real thing – so why bother? God was not likely to be interested.

The truth was that, as often happens, they projected their own fears and indifferences onto God. God was *intensely* interested in the rebuilding of the temple and would fill the new building with greater glory than the old. To counter the attitudes which had wrongly been attributed to God, God sent two prophets to argue his case. One was Haggai. The other, Zechariah.

With quiet logic, Haggai, Zechariah's older contemporary, asked the people to weigh up their position. If they did so they would soon realise that they were bringing ruin upon themselves. The only way out was to be up and building the temple. With gentle authority he inspired them to get up and do something.

Zechariah's approach was different. Firstly, he put before the people a series of visions that God gave to him (chapters 1–6). Then he preached a series of sermons on the themes of judgement and salvation (chapters 7–14).

The key to the visions, and the essence of Zechariah's message, lies in Zechariah 2:13, 'Be still before the Lord, all mankind, because he has roused himself from his holy dwelling.' God showed Zechariah that he was about to initiate activity in his world and establish his rule. The eight visions explain fully how he will set about doing this. Even though the meaning of the details may be uncertain in places, the main thrust of each vision is unmistakable.

God's four horsemen

'During the night I had a vision – and there before me was a man riding a red horse! He was standing among the myrtle trees in a ravine. Behind him were red, brown and white horses.

I asked, "What are these, my lord?" . . .

Then the man standing among the myrtle trees explained, "They are the ones the Lord has sent to go throughout the earth."

And they reported to the angel of the Lord, who was standing among the myrtle trees, "We have gone throughout the earth and found the whole world at rest and in peace."

Then the angel of the Lord said, "Lord Almighty, how long will you withhold mercy from Jerusalem and from the towns of Judah, which you have been angry with these seventy years?" So the Lord spoke kind and comforting words to the angel who talked with me.' (Zechariah 1:8–13.)

In the first vision Zechariah is in a peaceful grove of myrtle trees. There he sees a horse-rider despatching three others on an intelligence-gathering mission throughout the earth. They return to report that all is peace and happiness. But, in Calvin's words, it is 'an accursed happiness'. The nations are happy because they are not worrying about the way they are oppressing the Jews! Although God intended that his people should be punished, the nations have gone over the top and behaved with excessive vindictiveness towards them.

Now the time has come for God to step in. He will punish the nations who have abused their position and show mercy again to Israel.

This first vision announces, then, that the tables will be turned and justice will be done.

Four horns and four blacksmiths

In the second vision (Zechariah 1:18–21) four horns, which represent the nations who have been cruel to the Jews, are being dealt with by four blacksmiths. It is a comic picture. The horns come alive, as it were, and are being chased around the forge by the blacksmiths who have their tongs and hammers at the ready and are eager to plunge the horns into the fire and beat them into a different shape. The horns, which have been so proud, will now receive their come-uppance.

Zechariah portrays it brilliantly. 'The craftsmen . . . *throw down* these horns of the nations who *lifted up* their horns against the land of Judah . . .'

The second vision announces that God will be at work to reshape the nations. We may not think his agents – or 'blacksmiths' – work when we think they should, but work they will.

A man with a measuring line

'Then I looked up – and there before me was a man with a measuring line in his hand! I asked, "Where are you going?"

He answered me, "To measure Jerusalem, to find out how wide and how long it is."

Then the angel who was speaking to me left, and another angel came to meet him and said to him: "Run, tell that young man, 'Jerusalem will be a city without walls because of the great number of men and livestock in it. And I myself will be a wall of fire around it,' declares the Lord, 'and I will be its glory within.' " ' (Zechariah 2:1–5.)

The oppressors of Judah will be dealt with. But that is only half the problem. The people of Judah need to be re-established in their land and to rebuild their broken city. This vision concerns that process and the pessimistic voices raised as the early stages of reconstruction took place.

It is not clear whether the man was measuring the city to ensure that it was the same size as the old one, or, worse still, measuring it to complain that it was *smaller* than the old one! What is clear is that, either way, his vision for the future is far too limited. The new Jerusalem will be so vast that it will not be possible to put a wall around it!

So how will it be protected? How will it be made secure? ' " . . . I myself will be a wall of fire around it," declares the Lord, "and I will be its glory within." '

Zechariah rams the message home. The people need a greater vision of what God intends to do. They must renounce their fear and start exercising faith. Many of them have not even bothered to return to Jerusalem yet, feeling that it is not worth it. But if they do not return they will miss out. God is going to be there and do tremendous things among them.

Down the centuries the church has been dogged by the same cautious and fearful attitude which always wishes to measure the walls and test their strength. Bricks, mortar, money and prestige are the protective materials we can understand.

If the church is to grow it needs a vision like this vision of Zechariah. It will teach us to forsake the maintenance attitude to God's work and be inspired by how great his kingdom will be. It will help us not to look to material things for our security and to find it instead in the weapons of our spiritual warfare (Ephesians 6:10–18). It will show us that God will bring about his kingdom in any case, so we might as well be in on the act rather than left behind missing it all!

Clean clothes for the High Priest

Zechariah's visions do not breathe a spirit of glib triumphalism. If God is to do this new thing something has to be done to create a new people. The existing people, unless they are changed in some way, will only mess the new work up!

So attention turns to the priests who, as the people's spiritual leaders, are most to blame for their moral uncleanness and unpreparedness for God's work. Reform starts with them, and in particular with the High Priest as representative of the rest. Zechariah sees Joshua, the High Priest, in his vision. He is standing before God, wearing filthy clothes and Satan is accusing him of every sin in the book. But God rebukes Satan. He is not concerned with justice alone but with grace. He is the God who rescues those who cannot rescue themselves. To demonstrate the point God then commands that Joshua's filthy clothes should be peeled off him and replaced with clean, fresh ones that befit his office. Having had this miracle of mercy worked for him, the High Priest is charged to live up to God's requirements of him.

So Zechariah has a vision of a cleansed and obedient priesthood who are fit to serve in the new city of Jerusalem (Zechariah 3:1–7).

A gold lampstand and two olive trees

This vision (Zechariah 4:1–3) is the most difficult one to interpret in detail. It seems to be concerned again with the small-mindedness of the people.

Zechariah sees a gold lampstand with several wicks burning, supplied with a generous amount of oil from two olive trees, to keep it alight. By contrast with his contemporaries' limited vision, Zechariah presents a brilliant picture of the people of God: they are lights for the world. It is true that, judged by normal standards, they do not look very bright nor do they seem to have much to offer. But from God's perspective things look different. He has made them out of 'solid gold' and he keeps the fuel flowing directly to them without their being dependent on any human agency for supply. Their achievements will not come about through normal human resources: ' "Not by might, nor by power, but by my Spirit", says the Lord Almighty' (4:6). Human resourcefulness is not what matters.

The olive trees represent 'the two who are anointed to serve the Lord', Joshua the High Priest and Zerubbabel the king. Leaders have their part to play. But their part is secondary to the power of God in every one of his people as they are called to be lights in a dark world.

Again we have an inspiring vision. The people may have felt overawed by the size of the task facing them. What could they accomplish? Much, says the prophet, not because they were anything in themselves but because the Almighty God was with them.

A flying scroll

Zechariah sees a flying scroll (Zechariah 5:1–4). He is told it is a curse which God is sending out over all the land. It will 'enter the house of the thief and of him who swears falsely by my name. It will remain in his house and destroy it.'

This vision draws attention to two things. Firstly, sin must be dealt with in all the people, not just in the priests. Secondly, there can be no salvation without judgement. All cannot be just and right whilst injustice and wrongdoing are permitted to continue. We often want the salvation without the judgement but that is impossible even for God. And we dare not pretend otherwise in our preaching of the gospel.

A woman in a basket

Picture a large laundry basket being whisked up into the sky by two winged women and carried away far into the north. On the journey the occupant of the basket tries to escape. But she is kept firmly in place. There you have Zechariah's seventh vision. What does it mean?

The woman in the basket is the personification of wickedness. The evil that has to be removed does not operate on the level of the sins of individuals alone. Paul spoke of our spiritual warfare being 'against the ruulers, against the authorities, against the powers of this dark world and against the spiritual forces of evil in the heavenly realms' (Ephesians 6:12). Zechariah has a vision of God rousing himself to deal with those powers.

The basket is taken off to Babylon, the headquarters of evil, where it can trouble the people of God no longer. Of course, evil resists. She tries to escape and return to play havoc with God's people. But this time God keeps the lid on her. When it comes to it she is no match for him. God triumphs over evil. (Zechariah 5:5–11.)

Four chariots

The final vision is strongly reassuring and completes the picture. Just as at the beginning, so now scouts are sent throughout the earth to see what they can find. This time they return to report that the land is again at rest. But it is rest with a difference. This peace has been brought about by God's Spirit, not by the heartless cruelty of men who live in indifference to the plight of others. (Zechariah 6:1–8.)

Together, these visions gave Zechariah a powerful

picture of God at work. He had roused himself and established his kingdom. He would bring justice to the earth. He would restore and transform his people, making them great, secure, clean and powerful. He would deal with wickedness and bring real peace.

Zechariah was capable of preaching some plain and forthright sermons. But simply by using arguments he may never have inspired his people to wake up to the new day of opportunity which was in front of them. But if only they could capture his vision. . . !

We need down-to-earth, sober, practical people in the church. But we also need dreamers and visionaries. It is a mark of the age of the Spirit that they should have a place within the church (Acts 2:17–18).

There are two respects in which we particularly need them. Firstly, we need them to keep us going when situations seem far from promising. Many small, local churches seem all but dead and need a new vision of what God can do. My first pastorate was in a small church which once had only a handful of people for the evening congregation and wondered how long it could keep open. Things changed when two young couples joined them who had a vision that the work of God could grow in that place. They got stuck in and worked hard. Some years later God began to translate that vision into reality. That church is now growing and flourishing.

In some cases a vision is needed not just for individual churches but for whole countries. The continent of Europe is so spiritually barren that many men and women are needed to work there, keeping a vision before them of what God can do to revive his church again in the continent of the Reformation.

Secondly, we need visionaries who can point us to the future and stop our moans that what is happening now is not a patch on what used to happen in 'the good old days'. Have you noticed how all the great preachers always seem to be dead ones?! If God does a new work it will probably not be through the same organisations and meetings that he used years ago. He moves on and uses new groups, strategies and structures. New patterns, forms of fellowship, meetings and organisations will be generated and old ones left behind. Like the people of Zechariah's day we must not look back to the old 'temple' or structures and say that the new will not be able to reflect the glory of God as much as they did. What is to come is just as good, if not better.

Of course, there is nothing worse than a vision which is never fulfilled. Hope which is constantly disappointed is emotionally and spiritually damaging. Because of the element of risk, some people discount all dreams and visions, but that is to throw out the baby with the bath water. Instead we must ensure that our visions and dreams have their origin in the Holy Spirit, rather than in our own wishful thinking. With that in mind, let the dreamers dream and the visionaries have visions. We need them!

Take it from here . . .

- Take time to sit down and think what God might be able to do with you and your church if he had the chance. Let your imagination work – ask God to guide it.

- When you have caught sight of some of the possibilities for your situation check them against the ideas Zechariah had, to make sure that they are God's possibilities and not just wishful thinking.

- How can you get ready, and help others get ready, to bring those plans to fulfilment?

9

Malachi

Probing religious defences

The most difficult time of all in which to be a messenger of God is when nothing much is happening. If judgement is obviously at work, as it was in Joel's time, you can deliver a clear message and will find a responsive audience. If God has just worked some great act of deliverance, as in the time of Moses, people will be prepared to listen. But when times are quiet and nothing much at all seems to be happening, it is a different story.

It was at just such a time that Malachi was called to speak for God. Like several other servants of God we know virtually nothing about him. In fact, our knowledge of him is so limited that some suggest he did not even exist! Malachi means 'my messenger' and some have seen it as a convenient title for a book which speaks about God sending his messenger (3:1). Unlike many other prophets we do not even get a glimpse of his call at the beginning of the book. It is straight down to business.

The momentous events through which Israel had lived were now nothing but a memory. The exile had come and gone. The restoration of Jerusalem had taken place and the temple had been rebuilt. National life had been re-established. Even on the international front all was quiet. Routine had taken over and monotony had set in. A war, persecution of some sort, or a calamity might have been a welcome interruption! Better still, some windfall blessing which would assure Israel that God still loved them. Instead, God seemed to be keeping a very low profile. In fact, he seemed to have forgotten about them altogether.

How did the people react? Very much as we react today. Firstly they demanded that God should do something to prove he was still there and that he loved them. Secondly, they began to grow slack and nominal in their faith.

Malachi addresses the situation as if he were in a court of law. Israel's charge against God is spelled out in verse 1. 'How have you loved us?' they have been asking. Malachi then casts Israel as the defendant, whom God cross-examines relentlessly to show that the truth is very different from that which she perceives.

Israel had grown impatient with living by faith, sometimes just having to wait on God, and wanted to live by sight instead. 'If you love us,' they were saying, 'where is the evidence of it now? Don't simply point us to the past. It's *today* we're concerned about!'

God, however, cannot give in to them. He invites them to look to their past and recall how he has shown his special love for them. He chose them to be his people and history repeatedly confirmed his commitment to them. In the same way, he says, the future will also witness to his special love for them. In these quiet days, when life seems very ordinary, it is up to Israel to trust God without scepticism and serve him without cynicism.

God goes further, to point out that this is precisely what they had *not* been doing. Because God had been silent they had taken him for granted. They assumed his law did not mean what it said, so they had been cutting corners in worship. Suddenly the tables are turned and it is God who is cross-examining his people.

Insincere worship

'A son honours his father, and a servant his master.
If I am a father, where is the honour due to me? If
I am a master, where is the respect due to me?'

God begins with their worship. He points out that his
people would not have treated a human father the way
they have treated him. They have shown utter contempt
by bringing animals to sacrifice which were not good
enough for anything else, rather than selecting the very
best from their flocks and herds. The priests come in for
special mention. They were supposed to uphold standards and teach truth. Instead they have taught whatever
they liked – but it certainly was not the truth!

God comments that they may as well shut up shop
(1:10): 'Oh, that one of you would shut the temple
doors, so that you would not light useless fires on my
altar!' Not all religion is good religion; some of it is
actually a spiritual liability.

God is not concerned here about correct outward
ritual, but about what the outward ritual says about
the inward state of the heart. If they really did have a
relationship with God and if they really were concerned
about his great and glorious name then they would
certainly not be so casual in their approach to him.

Malachi hits the nail right on the head for our own
day. In our relaxed and informal days, which have
brought many positive benefits with them, there are
grave dangers. We go to worship when it suits us or
when we feel like it. We have little sense that the Sover-
eign Lord is summoning us and requires our presence.
We drift in, sometimes late; a thing we would certainly
not do if it was an appointment at Buckingham Palace!
We dress how we like and give whatever we just happen

to have in our pockets. Our minds wander as prayers are said and the sermon preached. We object to much of what happens and only join in with what suits us! It is all so man-centred that God hardly gets a look in. Is our worship falling under the same condemnation as that of Malachi's day?

What about 'priests'? Rather than standing for clear truth many of our church leaders are compromising on moral issues and fudging Christian doctrine. They are notorious for it and, sadly, see their uncertainty as a virtue.

God's judgement on such blemished worship is harsh. How can this square with a God of love? Elizabeth Achtemeier speaking of this problem reminds us that, 'It is only when he leaves us alone that he no longer loves us. It is only when he abandons us to our sin that we have fallen from his mercy.'

Broken covenants

Next, Malachi charges the people with breaking their covenant with God. This is reflected in their lack of integrity generally in day-to-day dealings and specifically in regard to marriage and divorce: 'Have we not all one Father? Did not one God create us? Why do we profane the covenant of our fathers by breaking faith with one another?' God had committed himself to them in a special relationship but they had proved disloyal by worshipping other gods. A fundamental lack of integrity in their relationship with God had led to the cheapening of their other relationships. God's command to them shows how closely the two are related: 'So guard yourself in your spirit, and do not break faith with the wife of your youth.'

People still lack integrity before God. But the issue is by no means limited to marriage. Our society is riddled with a lack of integrity and Christians bring great shame to their God if they connive with it. American television evangelists hit the headlines because of sexual scandals, bringing ridicule on the gospel. But we do not have to be in that league for integrity to matter. What about keeping our word, even if it proves inconvenient? Or delivering on our promises? We need to be transparently honest. If we believe the gospel we must live the gospel.

Corrupt 'justice'

The cross-examiner turns his attention next to the question of justice. The people were asking, 'Where is the God of justice?' and complaining that they could not find him. The truth of the matter, God suggests, is that they are looking in quite the wrong place! They have corrupted their value system to the extent that they now call good evil, and evil good. No wonder they do not recognise justice when they see it! But God promises to come to them: '. . . suddenly the Lord you are seeking will come to his temple' – but it will not be a cosy visit. He will come to judge those who doubt his existence. Their social ethics, economics, worship and social relationships will all be scrutinised.

People are still very quick to say, 'Where is God?' and demand that he comes to their aid. Again, like the people of Malachi's day, few realise the full implication of what they are asking. If God comes, he comes in perfect righteousness and that means that all our short-comings and sins fall under his condemnation. Would we then be so keen on summoning his presence?

Robbing God

Having despatched their complaint about the missing God, the cross-examiner raises a new charge: 'Will a man rob God? Yet you rob me.' The problem stemmed from their presumption that God should be giving to them all the time. They failed completely to appreciate that if God is God they should be giving to *him*. They were his servants, not *vice versa*.

Immediately the people protest: 'How do we rob you?' Apparently when the harvests had not been so great they failed to give God all that the law required by way of tithes and offerings. They put their own interests first – God could wait until there was a bit more in the bank. But God reminds them that it does not work like that. If they put him *first*, even if it seems foolish or costly, then they would soon find out that God would not fail them. This is no guaranteee of financial wealth. There is no automatic law at work. But it is a guarantee of a richness in one's relationship with God which will find expression in one way or another. Their cautious and calculating attitude towards money would prevent them from discovering what a rich and generous God he was.

Many of us today have the same difficulty. If we find ourselves in prosperous circumstances and a generous mood we will give to God. But if we are not so well off, God tends to be the first one to suffer. 'We can't afford to give', is what we sometimes say. But it is the reverse which is actually true: we cannot afford *not* to give!

I have frequently found that in my own experience. There have been occasions when I have argued with God about giving some gift and wanted to delay until times were more convenient. Yet the Holy Spirit has convinced me of the need to give and I have obeyed only to find that God in remarkable ways generously makes up for it. Sometimes this has been through receiving unexpected gifts myself, sometimes through the less tangible support of other Christians. But my relationship with God has deepened as a result.

Though the New Testament does not insist that we still give a tenth of our income to God a quick reading of 2 Corinthians 8 and 9 will soon show that the same spiritual principles are in operation. Although from the New Testament viewpoint the tithe is no longer a fixed obligation, perhaps it is still a good starting base.

Self-centredness

As a final assault, the Cross-examiner pitches in to the idea that it is futile to serve God if you get nothing out of it. The arrogant and self-seeking people seem to get all the luck and even the blatantly blasphemous do very nicely. What is the point of trying to serve God?

We have all felt like this at some time. It is, after all, what actually happens! Yet those observations reveal something telling about the question. Why do we not ask about what is right and what is wrong and ask instead about 'What's in it for me?' Those who were questioning God here were indicating that they would serve God provided they were happy with what he paid them for doing so. *They* reveal just as much of a commercial and utilitarian attitude to religion as the 'evildoers' they describe do to the rest of life. It is easy to go along with God as long as he answers our prayers, keeps us in good health and ensures our promotion at work. But the moment God disappoints us, do we turn our backs on him?

The prosecuting counsel's final statement

Some people in Malachi's day were different. A little group were faithful to God no matter what. These were the people who could see further than their noses, seeing that it was right to serve God regardless. In turn, God promised that they would one day be proved right. The prophet warns that a separation is beginning and only the 'remnant' who have been concerned to honour God will find him compassionate towards them.

At the end of his prophecy Malachi reveals the bottom line (4:1–6). The problem with those who have a calculating attitude to faith, and decide that it is not a good investment, is that they are making up their accounts too soon. The day of the Lord would come and would change everything. It would spell ruin to the prosperous wicked. Everything in which they had invested their security would be useless to protect them from God's judgement. What would they have then to boast about? Their only hope lay in turning back to God and in taking seriously his demands on their lives.

These were God's final words to his people for four hundred years. Malachi brought down the curtains on the old era. When it was to rise again it was to rise on the prologue of a new era.

Before 'the great and dreadful day of the Lord comes' God had promised to send a herald, a second Elijah. And after the long silence a prophet started preaching in the wilderness and preparing the way of the Lord. Following John the Baptist, Jesus came to announce that the day of the Lord had begun.

We are still living in those final days awaiting their consummation. The bottom line has not yet been finally drawn. But the pencil is poised.

Like Malachi, we have difficulty convincing people today that God has not absconded and that his day is coming. But we must make the effort. Perhaps Malachi gives us a clue as to how we might try to do so. Rather than being on the defensive and allowing people to attack authentic Christianity with the persistence of a gnawing toothache, perhaps we should turn the tables. It is time for us to cross-examine the nominal church and the world it represents in all its indifference to God and with all its self-interested lifestyle. Perhaps then we will find that it does not have so much to say for itself. Many might be less sure of themselves than they appear. And perhaps some will come to realise just how important it is to let God be God and man be man and not try to reverse the roles.

Take it from here . . .

- Are you ever too apologetic about your faith? How can you state your beliefs more firmly and with more conviction? If you need more convincing yourself, make time to read through a book which explains why the Christian faith is so reliable (eg *It Makes Sense* by Stephen Gaukroger, Scripture Union; or *This is Christianity* by Peter Cotterell, IVP).

- What aspects of the church do your non-Christian friends attack? How can you reply in a way which will give them a view of what *God* is doing, so helping them to see beyond the faulty institution?

- We often need to recapture a sense of God's importance. Ask him to help you do this.

10

John the Baptist
Being single-minded

We get slightly embarrassed about John the Baptist. He is a puzzling character and we are unsure what to make of him. He was far from conventional yet the people of his own day regarded him highly, realising that he was perceptive, full of integrity and spiritually powerful. (John 10:41). Jesus himself could not have spoken more highly of him (Matthew 11:11).

I like the statement of Campbell Morgan, quoted by J Oswald Sanders, about the greatness of John. 'How important the personality of John was considered, is seen in the manner Luke introduces him. One Roman Emperor, one Roman Governor, three Tetrarchs and two High Priests are all made use of to mark the hour in which the word came to John.' How's that for a fanfare to herald your arrival on the stage!

Given such an introduction, what has he got in common with the likes of you and me and how can his experiences help us? We can highlight two things. Firstly, his total devotion to God freed him from trying to fulfil the expectations of people. Secondly, he knew how important it was to give God all the glory and not to take any credit for himself.

Free from other people's expectations

John had been born to old and godly parents. They knew from the beginning that he was going to be something very special and, consequently, that he would be slightly unusual. I wonder what Elizabeth thought as she chatted to her neighbours about him. 'What's John doing these days, Elizabeth? Has he finished the synagogue school yet?' 'Yes dear,' she'd reply, 'he finished long ago and now he's living on his own in the wilderness, scratching together his meals from locusts and wild honey and dressed like a hippy. When he's going to start work I don't know!'

Perhaps she wouldn't have been as embarrassed as we imagine. For not only did she have fair warning that he was going to be different but she must have positively encouraged it. He may well have been brought up as a Nazirite, that is, one totally consecrated to God, who was not allowed to touch alcohol, nor to have his head shaved, nor to go near any dead bodies. That devotional discipline would have made him indifferent to what people thought about his dress or behaviour from early on in his life. Obedience to God was of far more importance than conformity to social convention.

His oddity continued into manhood, showing itself most in his dress and his diet. It also showed in his taking himself off to the wilderness, a place which many regarded with fear but which prophets regarded as ideal for communion with God. Furthermore it was the place where many thought the Messiah himself would appear (Matthew 24:26).

It was this total devotion to God which made him fearless not only in how he lived but in what he said. He did not mind who he was talking to. He would shoot straight from the shoulder. He never minced his words. Tax-gatherers and soldiers were singled out for special treatment but all were included under the blanket condemnation of a 'brood of vipers'. He clearly had not learned the art of diplomacy in the British Foreign Office otherwise he would have avoided the stinging rebuke he gave to Herod for his immoral behaviour. His fierce condemnations of immorality up and down the social scale were immensely disturbing to the *status quo*.

We spend a long time and a lot of energy ensuring that we win the approval of our peer groups. It may be most evident among the teenagers who all adopt the uniform of the latest fashion both in clothes and music and then deny that they, unlike their parents, are slaves to anyone! But the need to belong and to maintain ourselves in some group's approval-ratings never leaves us. It just becomes more conventional as we get older. So we do things, go places, drink liquids, buy products and adopt opinions to ensure that we will not offend and so risk rejection. John was free from all this, knowing that it was God's approval which mattered. Can we truly say that that is our motivating force in life?

Stepping out of the limelight

John was not only free and fearless but absolutely certain about his message. The time had come for God to do a new thing. The Messiah, so long hoped for, was about to arrive and he was to be none other than his cousin Jesus, from Nazareth.

In the face of this John constantly does himself down. The spotlight is directed fully onto the Messiah. John announces himself unworthy even to undo his shoelaces – an extraordinary statement to make about his own cousin. When Jesus came to be baptised by him, John resisted doing so, protesting his unworthiness for the task. You and I would have rushed to perform the ceremony and then boasted about it for the rest of our lives! He was content to be nothing more than a herald proclaiming Jesus' arrival.

Having said all that, John felt there was a need for him to fade still further from the picture so that Jesus might become more prominent. Rarely are we so caught up with Jesus as John was and rarely are we so willing to let Jesus have all the limelight. Somehow we always manage to engineer the light so that it falls on us, even if only just a little. But to be really effective as messengers of good news we have to learn the secret of John's humility. John's humility was no soft option. It did not mean he preached only a gentle, sentimental faith, nor did it lead him into a quiet, peaceful life.

Look at his preaching. It is radical. He does not call for a slight amendment of life, a touch-up job here and there. Rather he calls for demolition and rebuilding. 'The axe is already at the root of the trees, and every tree that does not produce good fruit will be cut down and thrown into the fire' (Luke 3:9). Half measures will not do. This is an all-or-nothing situation.

John demanded that people repent and was clear about how he expected them to show it. The wealthy entrepreneur was to give some of his possessions away. Ouch! The businessman was expected to start being honest. Impossible! Soldiers were expected to live with integrity and to start being content with their wages. Highly impractical! None of it was easy. It would make anyone who followed his advice a social nonconformist of a highly visible nature. But there was no room any longer for the *status quo*. The Messiah was going to upset it good and proper and if you wanted to prepare for his coming then this was the way to start.

We need to recover this understanding of repentance. At best we expect people to show a real sorrow for their sin. We might even expect new Christians to give up certain obvious sins like sexual misconduct or drunkenness. But today we do not expect repentance to have a social dimension to it. It does not go as far as challenging our materialism or making us radically different from our nice neighbours who are all on the fiddle or complaining about their wages. But it is not only the *status quo* of John's day that has to go if we want to 'make way' for the Messiah.

Alongside the genuine repentance which John expected to see manifested in people's lifestyles, was his command to them to be baptised. The ceremony was not new and it had some precedents in Judaism. But the meaning of this baptism was quite specific. It was a bath, a rather humbling and funny thing to do in public, which symbolised the washing clean from sin that repentance brought. This baptism was only in water; the Messiah would plunge people into his Spirit. But it was a right preparation for his coming.

The loser

Giving Jesus all the limelight had implications for John's own future.

John was an all-time loser. He had been too effective in his job as a signpost to Jesus. So when Jesus appeared on the scene, John lost his followers and his crowds, as they all went after Jesus. 'Everyone is going to Jesus,' said John's followers. 'He must become greater; I must become less,' he replied. John sounded magnanimous but I wonder if it hurt.

Having lost his crowds, he also lost his freedom. His lack of diplomacy finally caught up with him and Herod, holding a grudge for John's accusation against his personal immorality, locked him up.

In prison John seems almost to have lost his faith. Jesus turned out to be different from even his expectations. Like others, John expected the Messiah to bring in the imminent judgement of God, to speak with power and to baptise with fire. What Jesus was doing did not quite tie up. He seemed too slow, too gentle, too accepting. Jesus reminded John's messengers that what he was doing was exactly what the prophet Isaiah had foretold of the Messiah in passages like Isaiah 29:17–19 or 35:5–6. Yes, the 'servant of the Lord' *would* establish justice in the earth but like Isaiah's servant, 'He will not shout or cry out, or raise his voice in the streets. A bruised reed he will not break, and a smouldering wick he will not snuff out' (42:1–4).

Eventually John was executed. He paid the ultimate price for being a mere signpost for Jesus.

Jesus' evaluation of John was this: 'Among those born of women there has not risen anyone greater than John the Baptist; yet he who is least in the kingdom of heaven is greater than he' (Matthew 11:11). That puzzling statement was a fitting epitaph for one who deliberately tried to deflect attention from himself. He who made himself small was considered by his Lord to be great.

The fuller meaning of this curious tribute is that John played a strategic role in the history of salvation, that of herald of the Messiah, but that he belonged to the old era. He was essentially an Old Testament man. His bearing and his message underlined that. What he did, however, was to announce the arrival of the new era. And in the age of the New Testament even the least would be greater than John because the new way of relating to God was so superior to the old. Under the new covenant all were to be priests and prophets: all would have access to the Lord and all would be his messengers.

We have the privilege of being greater than John the Baptist! But to experience that greatness we must learn to be small before God. Only then will we have the courage to be bold in our witness and indifferent to the image-makers and the opinions of our society.

Take it from here . . .

- Think about it: how far have you allowed Jesus to challenge your lifestyle? If you really want to serve God you need to think about how you spend your money and your time so that you keep up with God rather than with your neighbours! Take time now to check out your way of living.

- John was completely devoted to God. How can you work at giving Jesus more room in your life? Ask God to show you.

- 'We spend a long time and a lot of energy ensuring that we win the approval of our peer groups.' Sometimes the effort can cause a good deal of worry and anxiety. Is there any particular area of life where your efforts to match up to other people's expectations of you are wearing you down? Ask God to release you from this and to assure you of his acceptance of you, just as you are.

11

Andrew

Forming an introduction agency

Andrew was never destined to hit the big time. Yet he was one of those vital people who play a secondary part in history with the result that they actually bring about events of great consequence. Without them the big time may never happen.

He was a fisherman from the town of Bethsaida on the north-east side of Lake Galilee who was inquisitive enough to go and listen to the preaching of the new prophet, John the Baptist. Perhaps he was curious to discover more about the God he already knew to some extent.

The Bible's portrait of Andrew is encouraging for all of us who have ever felt unqualified to be messengers of God because we could not preach or speak up in public meetings. Andrew never did either. He was a quiet, even diffident, man. He never stands centre-stage. Apart from three vital incidents in which his role is crucial, his name only occurs in the New Testament lists of those who were the original disciples of Jesus.

Those three incidents have one thing in common. In each of them we find Andrew introducing someone to

Jesus. He was not the sort to be the usher at a party, though, standing at the door and announcing the names as the guests come filing past! Rather, Andrew was the sort of person who waits for the right moment and then has a 'quiet word' in his friend's ear.

I know several people like him. One is John, a Geordie with a background in the merchant navy and the newspaper industry. One day his world collapsed around him. He was made redundant without notice and on returning home he found that his girlfriend's father had been taken seriously ill and she had gone to the other end of the country to visit him. Drink was his usual means of comfort but this time he made his way to a church, though he was not remotely religious. There he found love and encountered truth and, a few days later, came to Christ.

That started something! From that moment on he was introducing people to Jesus. His girlfriend was first and a few weeks later they were married and baptised. Everyone with whom John came into contact seemed to want to know more about Jesus whether they were newspaper editors and local businessmen, neighbours, shop assistants or those at the poorer end of town struggling to make ends meet on their fortnightly giro.

It was a relief to me when, the next year, John went off to Bible college. As his pastor, I could not keep up with the work this one-man introduction agency was generating!

Andrew and his brother

Andrew had heard John the Baptist speaking about Jesus as the coming Messiah. So he went to Jesus to judge for himself, and was convinced. The first person

Andrew introduced to him was his own brother (John 1:40–42) and that could not have been easy! Families are not usually the easiest to convince about new-found faith, and elder brothers, if that is what Simon was, are rarely willing to learn much from younger brothers! But we read, 'he brought Simon to Jesus'.

If Simon had interrogated Andrew he probably could not have answered all the questions and if discussion had developed he would probably have got his theology wrong. But then, he did not want to argue the matter himself. He was clear that what he had to do was to introduce his brother to Jesus. Once he had done that it was up to Jesus. But he seemed sure that Simon would immediately become a follower as well.

Back in 1875, Archbishop Tait objected to D L Moody's evangelistic campaigns because of their inadequate theology. But he was convincingly answered by the famous Congregational preacher R W Dale who said that 'whatever Moody's theory about repentance may be, his preaching leads men to repent.' In fact, he added, more people actually came to Christ through Moody's preaching than had ever done so as a result of all the dusty correct theological tomes in Lambeth Palace library. Andrew may have been comparatively ignorant about the faith but he still brought Simon to Jesus.

People who have only recently found Christ are often the best witnesses in the church. Their enthusiasm is natural and free. The discovery they have made is still fresh. Their minds have not been cluttered with problems and qualifications of the simple gospel. What is more they still have a great circle of 'pagan' friends because they have not yet been sucked into the church ghetto! As new Christians we may not always get our theology right and 'mature' Christians may sometimes blush at what they hear said. But that does not matter.

Bringing our friends to meet Jesus and become his disciples *does* matter.

Jesus immediately took command of the situation and a life-changing set of events was triggered, symbolised by Jesus giving Simon the new name of Peter.

Just think what followed from that simple introduction. Peter was to become not only the chief spokesman among Jesus's disciples but the chief apostle of the early church. Thank God for simple, straightforward introductions!

Andrew and a little boy

The second person Andrew introduced was a little boy (John 6:8–9). A great crowd, at least five thousand strong, had followed Jesus in order to hear him teach but also hoping he would do a few sensational things. That, combined with tetchiness at the end of a long hot day without food available, threw up the problem of crowd control. If they did not get something to eat it was likely that they would get restless, possibly violent. Recalling the way in which Moses had fed the Israelites in the wilderness, Jesus was to work another miracle to show that he was the prophet whom Moses had promised would come (Deuteronomy 18:15). But rather than simply doing so he wanted to stretch the faith of his disciples so decided to involve them in the miracle.

How could such a crowd be fed? Philip was simply stumped. It was impossible: 'Eight months' wages would not buy enough bread for each one to have a bite!' And who had eight months' wages to hand?

Andrew hesitantly ventured a solution. 'There is a boy here . . . oh, but it's no good. Stupid of me to mention it! He's got his lunch with him but what's the use of that? One lad's lunch isn't going to feed so many.'

But once again, the introduction had taken place. This time it was only a young boy that Andrew was introducing to Jesus and he was not at all sure why he had! But he was prepared to introduce anyone, and anything, which might be of use to his master. For all its deficiency, his reaction was less calculating and rational and more open and trusting than that of Philip. Underneath the insecurity there was an assurance that Jesus was quite capable of handling the situation.

This time, the result was a miracle. Over five thousand were fed from the simple rations of five loaves and two fish.

Andrew and a crowd of Greek people

The third introduction consisted of a crowd of Greek people (John 12:20–36) who had come up to Jerusalem for the Feast of the Passover and wanted to meet Jesus. They asked Philip for an introduction but he was not sure what to do. So he spoke to Andrew, almost as if Andrew was Jesus's minder. Andrew was in no doubt: there was no one whom Jesus would *not* want to meet. So he took Philip by the hand, metaphorically if not literally, and off they went to Jesus.

They must have been quite taken aback by the reply they received. Rather than saying either 'Yes' or 'No' Jesus started to talk about his 'hour' having come, about death and trouble. Then a remarkable disturbance happened in the sky. A voice – or was it thunder? – affirmed that God was right behind Jesus and, despite the trouble, would bring him great glory, greater even than that which he had experienced until now.

How did all that relate to Andrew's simple request?

It seems that the request had triggered an advance in the mission of Jesus. Jesus knew he had been sent to the Jews but now the Greeks wanted to see him too. It is true that his mission was eventually to be a universal one and that long-term it was never intended to be confined to the Jews. But before it took on that international dimension Jesus had to experience the agony of the cross. That lay between his present ministry and the Day of Pentecost. The request from the Greeks had brought that cross much closer, and with it the day when Gentiles would be able to share in the benefits of his mission as well.

So from these three simple introductions momentous things followed. In introducing Simon, Andrew links to Jesus the one who is to become the chief apostle. In introducing a little lad, Andrew initiates a tremendous miracle. In introducing the Greeks, Andrew triggers the passion and death of the Saviour and hastens the day when the whole world would be opened as a mission field.

Andrews since Andrew

You may not have heard of Edward Kimball or Maria Millis or Mordicai Ham. Yet these were the people who brought D L Moody, Lord Shaftesbury and Billy Graham to Christ. It is the unknowns – people like us – whom we have to thank for the world's famous preachers.

Andrew had the right aim. He knew that what people needed was to meet with Jesus. It was as difficult and as simple as that. Our aim must be the same. He did not short-change people with debate and philosophy. What they needed was the Messiah – a cure, a Saviour, forgiveness, wholeness and an ability to change their lives. And they could find that only in Jesus. So he was not going to stop short and offer them something less. Why is it that we can talk to people about all sorts of things, even about 'religion' and 'church', but seldom about Jesus?

Perhaps we have difficulty because we cannot say, with Andrew, that 'we have found the Messiah'. If our own experience is less certain than his then it is not surprising that our witness will be weaker. Not many people today jump out of baths and cry 'Eureka', as Archimedes apparently did, because few of us have made the discovery he did! His discovery is now an old and familiar truth and does not excite us in the way in which it did him. It can be the same with Jesus.

Perhaps we also have difficulty in talking of Jesus because we are not content to play second fiddle. A teenage boy will protest if he is only ever known as 'So-and-so's son' and is not credited with his own identity. A wife protests if she is referred to simply as 'So-and-so's wife'. Dennis Thatcher is forever labelled 'Margaret Thatcher's husband'. In Andrew's case he was most frequently known as 'Simon Peter's brother'. But he does not seem to have resented the fact that others got a greater share of the limelight. Maybe we do not introduce more people to Jesus because we are too busy introducing them to ourselves.

Perhaps we have difficulty in introducing people to Jesus because we lack Andrew's openness. We feel we have to defend Jesus and protect him. We do not want to trouble him with 'kids', or Greeks or people who do not 'fit' – people who are not, perhaps, 'nice' middle-class people like us. We prejudge the way Jesus will act or the way those people will respond to him. Perhaps we need to let go of our own ideas and just hand over to Jesus our inadequacies, like the loaves and fish, and the people who cross our paths, whether family or strangers.

Legend associates Andrew with more countries than almost any other of the apostles. It tells us that he not only lived by introducing people to Jesus but died for it too. He was no Peter, no Paul, not even a Stephen or a Philip. But just think how much would be missing if he had not been there.

If you are an Andrew, keep on with it! Introducing people to Jesus in a quiet way may not seem much. But out of it may grow a missionary, a miracle, or even a mission-field.

Take it from here . . .

- When people wanted to see Jesus, Andrew could bring people to see him in 'in the flesh'. How can you bring people to see Jesus today?

- What 'small people' are there in your life, people that others think are too insignificant to bother with? How can you bring them to Jesus?

- Who was 'Andrew' to you? Have you said 'thank you'? If you have not, do so if you can. Everyone needs encouragement, even great preachers!

12

A woman from Samaria
Being open to others

An innocent-looking carrier bag left at a bus station may well conceal a terrorist bomb. It is a sad fact of life that we have had to get used to. Things are not always what they seem. It is sometimes the same with 'innocent-looking' words in the Bible. Our ignorance of the context means that things which sometimes look quite ordinary to us ring warning bells with those who are more alert.

So it is with an innocent enough statement in John 4:4. 'Now', we are told, Jesus 'had to go through Samaria.' Jesus had been attracting more attention to himself than he needed at this early stage in his ministry and therefore withdrew from Judea, back to the quieter regions of Galilee. Samaria was *en route* and so it seems quite logical that 'he had to go through Samaria.' But, in fact, there was no 'had to' about it. For centuries the Jews and Samaritans had been at daggers drawn and relationships had broken down altogether in about 200 BC. Since that time Jews had gone nowhere near Samaria. If they wanted to get to Galilee they took the longer route, by-passing it.

So Jesus' route was not dictated by geography or custom but only by compassion and righteousness. By compassion because he was to meet there a lonely, hurting woman. By righteousness because it was time to bridge the racial divide. He 'had' to go through Samaria because God was calling him to.

The hurting woman

The woman to whom Jesus spoke, under the blistering heat of the noon-day sun, suffered, as far as any Jew was concerned, from a triple misfortune. She was a woman, a Samaritan and, since she had gone in for serial marriage, less than moral. No decent Jew would have touched her with a barge-pole. But Jesus constantly questioned the social niceties of his day and he deliberately went to find her and to talk with her so that she might find healing and life.

It does not take much to read between the lines. She was spiritually thirsty and emotionally unsatisfied (John 4:15–17). She had had five husbands and was currently living with a sixth man to whom she was not married. It may well not have been entirely her fault. The divorce laws discriminated cruelly against women. They could be rejected and thrown out on the streets without any means of support, almost at the whim of the man. A divorced woman had to find someone else to take her in. She would have had little choice in the matter.

She may well have been hungry for love. There may have been an aching heart within her. All her life she may have romantically dreamed of finding just that man who would love, cherish and support her, only to be disappointed by every relationship. Never mind, she may well have felt, next time it will be different. Another man enters her life. This time she is convinced it is the real thing. But she is disappointed once more. And so the aching void would continue and the compulsion to satisfy her thirst drive her down the same road again.

Less charitable explanations are also possible. It may be that she was simply immoral and created the problem herself. But there are no grounds for taking this line of interpretation rather than others.

Her conversation with Jesus reveals how she had learned, inadequately, to cope with herself. She had built up her defence mechanisms over time so that she had some means of protecting herself. She was not really able to handle conversation that got too personal. She could talk with Jesus about the differences in their culture ('Jews don't talk with Samaritans; so what's going on here?') and about practical things, ('You say you can give me water but you've nothing to draw it with!'). But when Jesus got too close to the bone she fended him off with an academic discussion on the validity of Samaritan, as opposed to Jewish, worship.

But all these are smokescreens. When we are hurting we are good at erecting smokescreens. It is a natural defence mechanism, a way of ensuring that a new relationship, or even an odd conversation, is not going to hurt us once again. Be hard. Keep your distance. Change the subject. Dismiss the real need as unimportant. Blame others. One way or another, up go the shutters.

The healed woman

The only problem is that such defensive reactions never allow the problem to be healed. It is only by dealing with the real issues, confronting them honestly, that healing can ever come.

So it was in the conversation between Jesus and this Samaritan woman. At first she may not have been able to cope with Jesus' exposure of her situation (John 4:17,18). But in the end, it was his gentle directness that unlocked the door and brought her release. Confronting the matter was what changed the situation. When she was able to face up to it she was able to find forgiveness and a deep acceptance and satisfaction in a new relationship with God. That would never have come if she had gone on running away.

Sometimes we hope that Jesus will let us off the hook for our past lives without asking deeper questions of us or dealing with the root causes of our problems. But it cannot be done. It will not work. The only way God can truly heal us is when we honestly admit our part in the failure.

David had to come to terms with this after his adulterous relationship with Bathsheba. Psalm 51 shows how he agonised over it but came to the point of saying, 'I have sinned.' The Prodigal Son was only able to put his life together again once he said 'I have sinned.' Proverbs 28:13 puts it like this, 'He who conceals his sins does not prosper, but whoever confesses and renounces them finds mercy.'

The honest woman

She hung on and listened to Jesus' confrontation. His exposing of her sin and of her need was painful, like cleaning a wound. But it also enabled her to be spiritually and emotionally healed. That healing turned her into a messenger of God. It is hard to suppress the news when God has really changed a person right around and dealt with years of pain and hurt.

John gives us four delightful insights into the Samaritan woman's witness.

First, she was enthusiastic; he notes that she left her water pot behind (John 4:28). She did not complete the job she came to do. More important things had taken over.

Secondly, she was honest. All her life she had been running away from the truth, and from herself. Now, at last, she was a woman of integrity. Without any of that earlier defensiveness she went back to the village and said, 'Come, see a man who told me everything I ever did!' The point is obviously significant since John repeats it. When the Samaritans could see her being *that* open they knew something must have happened!

Thirdly, she was humble. Rather than preaching at them she asked them, 'Could this be the Christ?' Having posed the question and aroused their interest by her own conviction about Jesus, they were left to draw their own conclusions. Perhaps that is a clue to effective evangelism. We can be a bit too keen to force our conclusions on people with the result that they remain *our* conclusions and are never really grasped by the people we are trying to win for Christ.

Fourthly, she was successful. She did not get hung up on trying to tell them the whole gospel. Rather, she aroused their interest to go themselves and listen to Jesus. They seem to have gone in droves! Her own testimony had been convincing but they found listening to Jesus himself irrefutable.

The role of the messenger is often to create an openness so that people will enquire further. Someone else, like a skilled evangelist or more experienced Christian, may then do the convincing. But creating the readiness in our friends to take that first step is vital.

A recent edition of *Moody Monthly* carried the story of Carol Rodgers. Her life was something of a modern parallel to that of the Samaritan woman, until Christ met her, too. Significantly, she too says that,

'Jesus confronted me with my sinful life, showing me everything I had ever done. Now all I wanted was him . . . Because of my past, however, I have been able to minister to many women who have had broken relationships. One woman was a lot like I was, thinking she could find fulfilment and love in a romantic relationship. I told her, "Give your heart wholly to Christ and wait on him to bring someone into your life because if you try to find love on your own, it won't work." '

There is a special witnessing role to be played by people whose backgrounds are full of hurts and of which they are not very proud. When Christ has dealt with the sin and brought them healing, they can speak with a special authority. They are often able to provoke even the hard and the indifferent to investigate Jesus more because of what they see he has done for them.

If you have a bruised and broken background but have let the Saviour release you, remember that your background does not disqualify you from being a messenger of God. On the contrary, it qualifies you in a special way to be an effective witness to him.

There is a special obligation laid on the church to reach such people. No one else will care for them. Our society only has time for the strong, the self-sufficient and the attractive. But if the church is to follow in the steps of Jesus it must obey God's call to 'go through Samaria'. This will mean going out of our way to meet those who are side-stepped by society. Our Samarias may be among the unemployed, the mentally ill, the emotionally damaged, the alcoholics or the AIDS victims. It also means that our words of reconciliation must be matched by our working to bring about reconciliation in the midst of racial and social hatred. Convention and sense may be against it, but God is most definitely for it. To avoid Samaria is to cease to follow Christ. It is to lack both compassion and righteousness.

Take it from here . . .

- How well do you listen to other people? Test yourself – how much can you remember of what a friend told you last time you talked? How often do you jump in with what is on *your* mind when a friend starts a conversation? Today, consciously practise *listening* when other people talk to you – you may be surprised at what you hear!

- Do you know anyone who is prickly, difficult to talk to? Listen hard, and see if you can get behind their abruptness to the person and the hurt that is making them difficult.

- If you have a friend who has been hurt by another person, by circumstances or by their own actions, what specific aspects of the good news of Jesus does he or she need to hear? Plan how you can share this with your friend during the week ahead.

13

Lazarus

Living the life

This man was a more influential messenger for Jesus than most, but he never said a word! His story can be an encouragement to many people, especially men, who feel their faith and devotion deeply but are not very sociable and find it very difficult to talk about it to anyone.

There was a family in Bethany, a town near Jerusalem, south-east of the Mount of Olives, who were close friends of Jesus. He had probably received hospitality there on a number of occasions. It consisted of two sisters, Mary and Martha, and their brother Lazarus. We know a lot of what the sisters thought, said and did, and quite a bit about their characters but we know nothing of what Lazarus might have thought, said or done, and even less about his character. Men are often less communicative about religious things than women. Even so they may still be messengers of God as Lazarus was.

There is only one reason he appears in the Gospel: he died. Jesus was warned that he was seriously ill. Obviously people knew he would be concerned and would maybe heal him. But he, in that mysterious way he sometimes had, did not go rushing to the bedside of his friend. He waited for him to die! When eventually he appeared at Bethany he listened patiently to the confused and upset rebukes of both sisters (John 11:17–32). Martha shows a greater readiness to understand than her sister Mary. Mary, as grieving people often do, simply expressed her anger, and blamed Jesus for what had happened. 'Lord, if you had been here, my brother would not have died.'

There was a divine strategy in it all which they did not immediately understand. It was not that Jesus did not care or love. He genuinely loved these people as his friends and was angered at the presence of death in his friends' household. But God permitted this to happen so that a great miracle could be done. Jesus wanted to show that the life-giving power of God was not reserved for some far-off day at the end of time, as Martha thought, but was very close to home. Furthermore, he wanted to teach that he was the one through whom resurrection and life were gained. All people had to do was trust him. And here was the evidence that he was worthy of that trust.

After four days in the tomb Jesus issued a death-defying order and commanded Lazarus to come out. Still bound in his grave clothes, Lazarus did just what he was told.

Overnight Lazarus became a sensation. People flocked to see him with their own eyes. Had he *really* been dead and was he *really* alive again? They had to see for themselves.

But Lazarus's new life was inextricably bound up with Jesus' life. People not only came to see Lazarus, they came to see Jesus as well. And John tells us that it was on account of Lazarus that 'many of the Jews were going over to Jesus and putting their faith in him.'

The sensation had its cost and again the fate of Lazarus was inextricably bound up with that of Jesus. The authorities decided they could no longer risk having Jesus do such things, and plotted to kill him. Steps were taken to ensure his arrest and execution. Jesus had to go underground for a time. They plotted the same fate for Lazarus too. He was also in the firing range.

What the eventual outcome was for Lazarus we do not know. The Bible is economical with its words so that we may focus on what is vital. Here the outstanding truth is that Jesus is the life-giver. The complementary truth is that those to whom he has given life can be irresistible, even if silent, witnesses to him.

Many non-Christians who will never go near a church will watch a believer they know at work and judge the truth of the gospel by him or her . . . Civil Servants, local government officials, businessmen and bankers, teachers, delivery men and labourers are all under the microscope for Christ every day of the week. And what you do matters. Alan Redpath tells as part of his testimony of the effect a godly man had on him when he was far away from God because the man took him out to lunch, did not preach at him, but left a good tip behind for the waitress!

I have lost count, thankfully, of the number of times I have heard people say of new Christians, 'We noticed a real change in him' or new Christians say, 'My friends have told me how much I have changed.' The change has always been worked by Jesus. He has taken the fearful and given them peace, the messed-up and straightened them out, the addicted and set them free, the dirty and made them clean, the damaged and made them whole. And when people see such real changes they ask their own questions and investigate further, just as the Jews did. The change of life speaks as powerfully as any words could ever do, if not even more powerfully.

Alexander MacLaren, the great Victorian preacher from Manchester, once preached a sermon called 'Wanted! A Lazarus.' He was right. The biggest need of the church is for people in whom Christ has done a visible life-changing work. Words then become less necessary.

Advertisers know that for all that they say about their products, the most effective way to sell them, if they are good that is, is to give away a free sample. We could do with a few less salesmen for Christ and a few more free samples! That is what Lazarus was.

Take it from here . . .

- Silent witnessing can sound like a cop-out, but there are many occasions when it is the *way* we respond to situations that impresses people, rather than our words. It is not always easy to respond in a Christian way. In what situations do you find it particularly difficult to behave as a child of God? Bring these situations to God and ask him to help you respond to them, next time they come up, with a confidence in him that will impress other people.

- Who do you know whose life has been changed dramatically by becoming a Christian? What message does this give you about Jesus? How can you share that message with others?

- Think of all the ways in which God has changed your life. Thank him for this message to you of his love. Ask him to help you share it with others.

14

Some women disciples

Risking everything

Perhaps the most surprising messengers of God in all history were a group of frightened women who were the first, early one Sunday morning, to receive the news that Jesus had risen. They were given the privilege of also being the first, apart from the angelic messengers, to announce that news to the world.

We cannot be sure of all their names, although we can identify Mary Magdalene, Joanna, the wife of Herod's household manager, Mary, the mother of 'James the less', Susanna and Salome. But whether there were any others who are not named we do not know. We cannot be sure of all their personal details but even so we can piece together a fair bit of information about them from what the Gospels tell us.

They were women for whom Jesus had done something very special. Luke tells us that, until Jesus came on the scene, their lives were being ruined and their personalities damaged – some of them by evil spirits (8:2). Luke leaves it as a general statement so we can only speculate exactly who was affected by demons and to what degree, and how they manifested themselves in the women's lives. But it would inevitably have made it difficult for people to relate easily to these women. Life for them would have been on the downhill slope.

But Jesus set them free. He often healed people by exorcism. It was central to his mission to cast out spiritual powers which had usurped the place that belongs to God alone in people's lives. And only after such deliverance could life be rebuilt on wholesome lines.

Their devotion

They repaid Jesus by being among his most devoted followers. Jesus once told a story (Luke 7:40–48), maybe in reference to one of them, about two men who owed money. One owed a lot and one not so much. But both were forgiven. 'Who,' asked Jesus, 'would show the most appreciation and love?' The answer was obvious. It was the one who had been forgiven much. The women were among those who experienced God's grace in no small measure so it was not surprising that they should have become so attached to Jesus.

Their devotion led them to keep up with Jesus as he went from town to town, in order to provide the practical support he needed – food, money and shelter. We must assume that they were relatively independent and had some degree of wealth themselves, for they seem to have supported him gladly. They are the first of many independent and perhaps therefore more affluent people down the centuries who have used the opportunity of being free from family responsibilities and economic pressures to support the work of Christ generously.

The devotion lasted to the very end. It took them miles from home to the strange territory of Jerusalem where, whilst others ran away, they stood at a distance and watched the gruesome final events of the crucifixion of the one they loved. The Gospels make the point that they had travelled with Jesus all the way from Galilee. Having come that far they were not going to desert him now, in what seemed to them his concluding tragic hours. They watched and wept. They must have felt angry and bitter that the world could destroy a life which had been so beautiful, silence lips that had spoken such wonderful truth, mutilate hands which had brought healing to so many and snuff out a life that had cared so much. They must have thought that darkness reigned.

At least they had the memory that it was not always so. They knew, from their own experience, that there was at least a brief time when Satan was defeated and people set free. Was it to be only a memory? Occasionally we meet people who can look back on some period of glorious spiritual experience but who are now in the depth of depression and nothing spiritual is real to them any more. Salvation and victory are only memories. But God does not intend it to be so. We know the end of the story in a way that these women didn't. Easter Sunday followed. Darkness was defeated once and for all and we must live by faith in that great fact whatever our feelings tell us.

Their courage

Their devotion was extremely courageous. Tacitus, a Roman historian who lived in the first century AD, tells us that it was dangerous for the friends and family of one being executed for sedition to be seen watching the execution, weeping at the death or following to the tomb. They might be made to suffer the same punishment. But these women were indifferent to any threats.

They were not only at the cross but also noted which tomb Jesus was buried in. As soon as the law permitted, they went there to anoint his body. They had attended to his needs during his life, they intended to do so now in his death. We cannot fail to note that the men showed no such courage. They ran away, or denied that they were associated with Jesus. With the exception possibly of John, it seems that only the women remained loyal to the end. Most of us are not called to put our loyalty to the test in such an extreme way. Even so, there are many little occasions where we can either identify with Christ or distance ourselves from him such as when the subject comes up at work. Do we show courage or loyalty then?

Whether they were confused by the jumbled emotions brought on by the events, or simply determined to find a way to get to Jesus' body in the tomb, we cannot be sure. But they seem to have missed out a few vital details in their preparation, like who would move the stone back from the grave for them to get in. Perhaps in their grief they had not been aware that arrangements had been made by the Jewish authorities to seal it securely and even post a guard outside it.

Their reward

It did not matter. When they arrived they were startled to find the grave open and messengers from heaven ready to announce the good news that Jesus had been raised from the dead. God, in response to their love, made sure they were the first to hear it.

Meeting angels was no more common an experience then than it is now. Moreover, the brutality the women had witnessed, and the grief they were suffering, left them in an intensely disturbed state. So they did not greet that first Easter day with relief and praises to God. We are told they were bewildered and afraid. Mary turned over in her mind other possible explanations of why the body was not there. Perhaps someone had moved him elsewhere. But eventually the most incredible news that history has ever heard sunk in. Jesus was alive again.

With their emotions tugging them in different directions – fear and joy flowing though them together – they went back to the disciples and told them the news. Were they believed? Not at all! The disciples were both typically Jewish and typical male chauvinists. They thought the women had gone gaga. They had really flipped. It was senseless women's talk. The law actually stated that a woman was not to be trusted and could not expect to have her testimony taken seriously. Obviously, if God wanted to communicate such an important message to the world as the resurrection of Jesus he would not do so through women! It would never be worth the risk. The message might get lost for ever . . . Or would he?

Perhaps, in this small detail of the resurrection story, God confirms the end of the old era and the beginning of the new. In the new age, 'there is neither . . . male nor female, for you are all one in Christ Jesus' (Galatians 3:28). Women have a part to play as witnesses too. Certainly he is pointing out once more that he can use the most surprising people, even when they are not quite thinking straight, as his messengers. We do not have to be all straightened out and fully acceptable to others to be of use to him. It never ceases to surprise me how some mixed-up people whose theology is anything but straightened-out are used by God to bring their friends and acquaintances into contact with the church and so through the church to Jesus. It sometimes even makes for a few pastoral nightmares ('Not another needy person, Lord? Aren't there any normal ones you want to save?'). But that's the way God works.

The special one

Matthew, Mark and Luke are remarkably consistent and realistic in what they tell us of these privileged messengers. John adds a further scene which is equally full of human realism. He alone records the conversation which took place between Jesus and Mary in the garden (John 20:10–18). It was typically gracious of him to appear to his distressed and perhaps most devoted follower in this personal way. It was with his typical gentleness that he spoke her name.

Her natural instinct was to reach out and cling to him. Wouldn't you have done the same? But 'Jesus said, "Do not hold on to me, for I have not yet returned to the Father. Go instead to my brothers and tell them, 'I am returning to my Father and your Father, to my God and your God.' " ' (John 20:17.)

What did Jesus mean? Just this. Devotion must never turn into sentiment. We can try to hold on to Jesus in the wrong kind of way. We can do so in a possessive manner which wants him to bring comfort to our own souls and nourish our own feelings. But that can be self-indulgent. The resurrection means there is a job to be done, a journey to be undertaken, a message to be spoken. Others need to hear the news. Jesus needed to ascend so that the Spirit might be given so that, in turn, the news would be announced around the world.

So much devotion is of the kind that wants to hold on to Jesus, to cling to the memories of the past and stay with the physical appearance of Jesus. But if we want to express true devotion to Jesus we will do so by spreading his message not by clinging to him for our private enjoyment.

We cling to Jesus in all sorts of ways. For some of us it takes the form of a dogged adherence to traditional patterns in the church, at the expense of reaching people with the gospel today. For others, it shows itself in our desire not to be disturbed in our own devotions by being made aware of the needs of our nasty and violent world. Even recent forms of worship or of celebration can be a way of clinging to Jesus as it makes us feel good to be in the warm cocoon of our fellow believers and means we're too busy to get stuck into the mission of the risen Christ and to be involved in evangelism or social problems.

Have we the depth of devotion which was to be found in Mary and the other women? We can easily measure it: are we prepared to use our resources – our homes, time and money – for him? Are we prepared to go out of our way for him, or do we adopt the easier option of not getting involved, leaving the work, the caring and the practical details to others? Are we prepared to identify with him as he is crucified? Are we prepared to overcome the obstacles, often no more than our own apathy, like the stone at the tomb's mouth, in order that we might anoint him? Are we prepared to say with Mary, 'I have seen the Lord' and witness to his resurrection, even though people may not believe us?

If not, it perhaps suggests that we have not yet realised how much he has forgiven us. We might be taking his forgiveness for granted or assuming that we have not done that much wrong for which we need to be forgiven. The more we realise how many of our spiritual debts he has cancelled, the more, like these women, we will love him.

Take it from here . . .

- Are you financially independent? That is, in a position to support other Christians with your money? Look over your resources and ask God to show you how to use them for him.

- Are you independent in strange situations? It is easy to feel insecure when we are in unfamiliar surroundings. What makes you feel uneasy? How can you help yourself to feel at home with God whoever else you might be with?

- Are you independent of sentiment? 'Devotion must never turn into sentiment. We can try to hold on to Jesus in the wrong kind of way.' If you go to a celebration service one Sunday night what are you like on Monday morning? How can you take God's presence with you into your daily life?

15

Luke

Telling your story

The thought of even holding a conversation which directly witnesses to Christ scares some people to death. Does that mean that there is no way they can be messengers of good news? No. God communicates in a whole host of ways and has given his people a range of gifts which can be used as the medium for his message: art, music, drama, mime, history and stories.

A creative approach

We all love stories and know they are a good way of getting a message over. The story sticks long after the abstract idea has left us and we have fun telling the same ones over and over again. The tradition of our churches tends not to encourage our telling of stories too much. Preaching which is often quite theoretical tends to dominate. But perhaps it should not when the best remembered part of the service is usually the children's talk in the form of a modern parable or story!

A friend of mine knows he will never make a great preacher but he has a desire to communicate the love of God, especially to children, and often through them to their parents. Because he is a school teacher he does not find it difficult to enter into the world of children and with a little imagination it is not long before he can spin a yarn full of spiritual insight. God has used him greatly as a messenger in that way.

Dr Luke was a man with just such a gift. His stories were true, not fiction, and he made sure that he had carefully checked their accuracy (Luke 1:3). Yet he was much more than a careful historian. He was also a superb story-teller. So it is not surprising that he records more of the parables and stories of Jesus than the other Gospel writers and retells them with beautiful simplicity. Think for example of just one of his stories: that of the Prodigal Son (Luke 15:11–32). He alone records it. And with what skill! Not only does he paint the scene with deft brush strokes but he evokes a variety of emotions as the tale unfolds. And then he leaves you with a cliff-hanger: did the older son go in to enjoy the party? We do not know. And we do not know for one very good reason: Luke has put *us* into the shoes of the older son and we have to complete the story by deciding what *we* are going to do!

Luke does not use abstract propositions to teach truth, but tells one story after another. Here is a story of what Jesus did. There is a story which Jesus told. Here is a story about someone in the early church. There is a story of something that happened to Paul. He lets the story speak for itself. His approach is a little different from the typical children's address where the moral is tacked on at the end to make it obvious. He does not need to do it that way because his stories carry their own message. 'Making the point' can sometimes dull the impact of an otherwise powerful story of what God has done.

God used stories to get points across to his people. Biblical history is one long story of his dealings with them, and most of us find it easier to learn from this approach than from statements about the truth.

A radical message

Reading Luke's writings, it soon becomes evident that he has some special concerns to get over. He talks much of prayer and the Holy Spirit, of joy and praise and forgiveness. He is down to earth and obviously lives in the real world. Perhaps that accounts for his frequent references to money! After all that is what occupies most of us most days! Above all he shows a special interest in people, even children, women and the socially deprived. These all figure prominently as the central focus of God's love. But there is more to it than first meets the eye.

As you piece together Luke's special concerns and note the slant he gives to familiar stories it becomes obvious that he is not a Walt Disney artist, simply aiming to produce a nice warm feeling inside his audience. His writing is politically, socially and economically radical; some would say subversive. There is a strong revolutionary fist in the smooth glove of the story-teller.

This strain in Luke's writings is evident right from the very beginning. Take, for example, the Magnificat. There, God is extolled as one who scatters the proud, brings down rulers, lifts up the humble, fills the hungry and sends the rich away empty (Luke 1:51–53). The Gospel then provides an illustrated commentary on the way in which Jesus does just that in the reality of everyday life. We could give numerous other examples, not only from the Gospel but equally from the book of Acts where Luke shows that God has every intention of turning the ways of the world upside down. All this is very disconcerting for those in the establishment.

When we begin to appreciate Luke's stance we cannot fail to be surprised at how much the church has today identified *with* the establishment. We have so often adopted the world's ways and deodorised the message of the gospel. Then we have seen Luke through a cosy filter that has reassured us that we are OK. I do not suppose Luke would be too pleased. If we want to live out the truth of his message we must take this disturbing element of the gospel seriously and not allow our stories to sentimentalise the love of God.

Luke, the creative writer

What do we know of this man who wrote over a quarter of the New Testament and has exercised such a great influence on the subsequent history of Christianity? He never takes the centre of the stage and is only mentioned explicitly three times in the New Testament (Colossians 4:14; 2 Timothy 4:11 and Philemon 24).

From subsequent writings we can build up a fairly accurate picture of Luke and this picture makes him all the more human. He was a Gentile, most likely born in Antioch of Syria. He was skilled in the Greek language and writes with superb artistry. He was a physician. Paul tells us as much in Colossians 4:14 and it seems amply supported by the precise vocabulary he uses when writing of diseases and healings.

One source, a prologue to the Gospel, written between AD 160 and AD 180, tells us that he was single and so was able to serve the Lord 'without distraction', having no wife or children to look after. That enabled him to travel widely and accompany Paul on many of his journeys. We can tell when he was with Paul and his companions from the way in which he switches from talking about 'they' to 'we' as, for example, he does in Acts 16:8 and 16:10. It seems that he stayed with Paul throughout his final imprisonment and attended to his needs. Another Prologue also tells us that he died in Boeotia at the age of eighty-four, 'full of the Holy Spirit'. This information also seems trustworthy.

Other writers have left more speculative suggestions about Luke. Among them are that he was the brother of Titus; that he was a fellow student with Paul at the University of Tarsus and that he may have been a freedman because, in Greek, his name ends in *as*, which was a common ending for the names of freedmen.

Getting the facts right

Luke himself tells us why he wrote his two-volume account of the work of Jesus: the Gospel and Acts. He admits that there were already many other accounts of the life and teaching of Jesus and that these were based on eye-witness reports. Why then the need for another? In the opening words of his Gospel he explains why. 'Therefore, since I myself have carefully investigated everything from the beginning, it seemed good also to me to write an orderly account for you, most excellent Theophilus, so that you may know the certainty of the things you have been taught' (Luke 1:3,4).

Luke's account was based on solid research. He had 'carefully investigated everything'. He was not himself an eye-witness to the life of Jesus but he had checked out the evidence with those who were and cross-checked their stories to get to the truth of the matter. And he had consulted earlier written evidence too.

There was a time when scholars were doubtful about Luke's reliability and accuracy as a historian. But research has shown that Luke is thoroughly reliable. Archaeology and studies in Roman law have given credence to his writings where doubts were once cast.

In this respect Luke is a good model. Before we talk of Jesus or of what God is doing today we should be sure that we have a solid foundation for what we say. It is easy for testimonies to get embroidered as they are told and for claims to be made which do not stand up to closer investigation. This doesn't lead our hearers to Christ, but only to becoming disillusioned, doubting the truth of whatever we say about him!

Luke's account was also 'an orderly account'. That is evident both in the Gospel and the Acts. He has organised his material on a tidy framework to help his readers understand it. In Acts the framework is mentioned in chapter 1 verse 8: the book will tell the story of the expansion of the church from Jerusalem through Judea and Samaria to the ends of the earth.

Luke also tells us that he wrote both books for the 'most excellent Theophilus'. Who Theophilus was is one of the most intriguing and unresolved riddles of the New Testament. It is likely that he was a young believer who needed instruction and encouragement in his faith. But it could be that he was not yet a believer, only an enquirer. His title suggests that he was probably of high social rank. We can be sure that, like Luke, he was also a Gentile. Many things in these two books make them eminently suitable for a Gentile audience. Luke constantly stresses the breadth of God's love for the world and presents him as breaking out of the narrow confines of the Jewish people.

Lastly, the opening verses of the Gospel tell us that Luke wrote to Theophilus 'so that you may know the certainty of the things you have been taught.' If Theophilus was a believer it seems that there were several things which were shaking his infant faith. The church was far from perfect, persecution abounded and the kingdom was perhaps not being ushered in with the obvious power which he had anticipated. If he was only an enquirer he may well have had discussions with Luke as to whether there really was any solid basis to this new faith. Either way Luke is concerned to say to Theophilus that the faith of Christians was built on a firm foundation. He was not believing a myth, a fairy story, or a set of half-truths which had been imaginatively embroidered, but solid truth and attested facts.

When Luke begins his second volume, he has clearly not forgotten his aim. Writing of the resurrection he says that Jesus 'showed himself to these men and gave many convincing proofs that he was alive . . . over a period of forty days' (1:3,4). There is, he says, convincing evidence that Jesus is risen.

The result of Luke's research was that he wrote the most comprehensive narrative that we have of the origins of the Christian church. It is far more extensive than any other Gospel and it is unique as a record of the life of the early church. It stretches from the announcement of the birth of Jesus to the final days of Paul. It reaches from an obscure village called Bethlehem to the centre of the known world, Rome. And it is one continuous account of the activity of Jesus, in the flesh and in the Spirit.

Today's Lukes

Luke was not a professional theologian or priest. He was just a medical doctor who had a skill in writing. I suspect that if you had put him in front of a large congregation and told him to speak he would have clammed up! But God spoke through him around the world and down the generations, using the gifts he did have rather than the ones he might have had. And God can do the same through you.

If may be the gift of telling stories, or of using drama or music. A young man I know has an ability to mime, which he uses to convey his message with precision. He manages to rivet the attention of his audiences more than any preacher I have seen. And he does not say a word! What he does do is to use his gift for Jesus.

The evangelical church has often been sceptical about 'the arts' and discouraged its members from developing their talents in those areas. God apparently has no such qualms. The writing of good literature, the telling of exciting stories, the use of contemporary parables, the recording of *lively* history and the telling of our own 'stories' of what God has done for us communicate the good news with radical and refreshing vitality.

Take it from here . . .

- Luke had a talent for telling stories. What creative talents – music, drawing, singing, dancing, writing – could you be using for God, and how?

- Check what you say to people about your experiences of God. It is easy to start exaggerating for the sake of a good story! Make sure that any stories you tell about yourself *or others* are true, and relevant to those listening.

- People often challenge Christians about the historical basis of their faith. If you are not sure how you would reply to such a challenge, do some finding out about the accuracy of the Bible. Books of Bible background will help you here (eg *The Lion Handbook of the Bible*).

16

Stephen

Living dangerously

It was a peaceful Saturday evening and I was half listening to the television news whilst writing some letters.
Suddenly a face came on the screen I thought I recognised. There was Mary Fisher, a woman who had been
a fellow student with me at London Bible College some
years before, now serving God as a missionary nurse in
Africa. The letter writing was soon forgotten and I listened with growing shock as the news item unfolded. The
mission station where she worked had been attacked
and a number of missionaries killed. Mary was still alive
but badly injured and struggling for her life. In fact
she lived a week and died on the morning of LBC's
Graduation Day in 1978. Commissioning students to
serve Christ in such a world of violence had a special
meaning that year. I could not get over the fact that I
had studied alongside a future martyr. Who knows how
many others might have to pay such a price for their
faithfulness to Christ?

There have been more martyrs this century than ever
before. Some, like Jinani Luwumb, the Archbishop of
Uganda who stood up to Idi Amin, may have been men

of prominence. Some of them, like Luwumb and the first-century deacon Stephen, have run into trouble because they have opposed the established religious or political ideologies of their day. But all of them, if you had been able to ask, would have denied that there was anything special about them. They were quite ordinary and not given to special courage or foolhardiness. Mary Fisher had been remembered for her godliness when she was a student. She was lovely. But she was also quite quiet and, if I may say so, quite ordinary. She was not, you would have thought, the stuff out of which God makes martyrs. But it is people like us that God chooses, even for martyrdom.

Nothing by halves

Stephen was a Hellenist, that is, a Grecian Jew. Many of them had joined the church and were considered by the rest to be second-class citizens because they were not pure Jews from the homeland. Like many others with a similar background he worshipped at the Synagogue of the Freedmen and it was there that the trouble began.

In telling us his story Luke emphasises that Stephen was Christ-like and Spirit-filled. Perhaps Luke realised how important it was to stress that, otherwise we might dismiss Stephen as a dangerous radical who got his just deserts.

When the apostles decided that it was right to set up an alternative leadership within the church who could take the practical needs of the Hellenist converts seriously it was Stephen who was the first to head the list of nominations. His qualifications were not that he was a practical man and a good administrator but that he was 'full of faith and of the Holy Spirit' (Acts 6:5). We do not know how he fulfilled his specific task of caring for the Greek-speaking widows in the church, though, because other issues take over and Luke tells us immediately about his evangelistic work.

Stephen clearly did nothing by halves. The very next reference to him uses the word 'full' again! This time we are told that he was 'full of God's grace and power'. In other words he must have been very like Jesus. His preaching was certainly full of Jesus and when on trial there was something about even his appearance which was quite remarkable: 'All who were sitting in the Sanhedrin looked intently at Stephen, and they saw that his face was like the face of an angel.' Perhaps he reminded them of an earlier trial that some of them had witnessed, that of Jesus himself.

It should not surprise us that wherever Jesus is involved the Holy Spirit is mentioned too. The Holy Spirit is the *alter ego* of Jesus. It was not only Stephen's character which was full of the Holy Spirit; his work was too. The Holy Spirit had put his mark upon him in an exceptional way. When he spoke people may not have accepted what he said but could not argue back against such irrefutable wisdom. And since 'the kingdom of God is not a matter of talk but of power' (1 Corinthians 4:20) we see the Holy Spirit working through Stephen not only in his speech but also in his actions. He did 'great wonders and miraculous signs among the people.'

Provoking a reaction

It never ceases to surprise me how many people hate what is good. In the first church I pastored a number of teenagers were converted, to the alarm of their parents who often gave the impression that they would have preferred it if their children had hung around on streetcorners or put bricks through shop windows! Then I think of a woman who became aggressively opposed to her elderly mother (whom until this time she had been neglecting) once the old lady linked up with a lively church and found her isolation overcome by the fellowship it offered.

True to form, far from being welcomed as a man who had the ability to put matters right through miracles and healing, Stephen provoked opposition. John was only too right when he said, 'men loved darkness instead of light'. Preachers of truth, doers of kind deeds and workers of miracles should not expect to receive a welcome in this world!

Stephen's ministry, however, was not one to provoke discomfort in a general sort of way. It had a cutting edge to it. He was the sort of person you either loved or you hated but could not be indifferent about. You could not sit on the fence; he forced you to conclusions. And it was this ability, which we so often shun in the church today, that led him to be tried in the supreme court on a charge of blasphemy and to receive a capital sentence.

The charges were trumped up and false witnesses had to be brought in to make them. The same strategy is used today around the world against courageous church leaders who speak out clearly and uncomfortably for Christ. Christian civil rights leaders in America and Christian pastors in South Africa constantly face harassment through false charges of adultery. There are pastors behind the Iron Curtain who can never drive alone in case the secret police engineer an accident and attribute the blame to them, with trial and prison as a result. Smear campaigns and outright injustice – even in this country – are not uncommon where people are prepared to speak out for Christ in plain words.

Nonetheless, as Stephen stood in the dock he transformed it into a pulpit to proclaim his message. And that is another thing in common with today; many an oppressed person, like Ghandi, Biko or Mandela have done the same. We should not be intimidated when people try to put us down because of our faith. Instead we should take the opportunity to turn the tables and to say something positive for Jesus. Stephen's defence was powerful, accurate, theological, radical and pressed home. No wonder his accusers wanted to dispose of him!

Getting the point across

Stephen was in no way discourteous. He began by respectfully addressing those assembled to hear the case as, 'Brothers and fathers'. Then for some time it sounded as if all he was doing was giving them a history lesson from Abraham onwards, telling them what they already knew too well!

But this was not just a history lesson; his hearers were on the edge of their seats. The recital of Israel's history pointed clearly to the fact that God had rejected the holy land, the holy city, the holy temple, the holy rituals and the holy law as ways to God and had provided a new way of direct access.

Then he turned the knife. God's people, he said, have always rejected God's words and messengers – and they have just done so again. This time it was not just any old prophet that they rejected but the 'Righteous One', Jesus Christ, the new way of access to God.

Enough was enough! The supreme court had heard sufficient to establish a charge against him, and sentence was passed.

Here again Luke is concerned to draw lines of comparison between Stephen and Jesus. They were tried on the same charge of blasphemy and received the same sentence, although the prosecution of the case against Stephen was more straightforward than that against Jesus. As Stephen was led out to be stoned the ascended Jesus revealed himself to him. Stephen kept his eyes firmly fixed on Jesus and he died repeating the words that Jesus himself had used on the cross: 'Lord, do not hold this sin against them.' In the face of such a horrendous method of execution Luke can calmly comment, 'When he had said this, he fell asleep'. Jesus had once and for all altered his followers' perception of death by their knowledge of his own resurrection.

Is there room for Stephens today?

I doubt that Stephen would be too welcome in some Christian circles. He would be too radical, too impatient, too impolite. He would be told to 'quieten down', to 'see both sides of the argument' and not to reject tradition in 'so cavalier' a fashion. The brilliance of his argument would not be appreciated. He would be judged 'too clever by half' by many people who simply want the reassurances of their folk religion. The church has a long history of ejecting such uncomfortable people. It happened to Martin Luther, John Wesley and more recently William Booth who, having been told by his Methodist friends to take a more measured approach to religion, left them and eventually founded the Salvation Army. Still today, we have little room for clever people or strong leaders and go for the lowest-common-denominator type of leadership; one that is good at 'keeping everyone happy'. Stephen did not.

The church needs to wake up. We need the dangerous radicals like Stephen though their names may never reach beyond their own fellowships, to help us do so. We have a radical message: Jesus is the new centre of faith! But law, tradition, buildings, rituals and memories, *the very things against which Stephen was speaking*, often seem to be the true centre. How can it be that such a world-defying faith as that of New Testament Christianity can have settled down to such compromise with the world and be so complacent? Why is it that if we are militant about anything we are militant about *blandness?*

It is almost shocking to realise that this most radical of all New Testament preachers is the one who is most explicitly identified with Jesus. His disturbing habit of going for the jugular may not go down too well in our polite assemblies but it does not seem to have distanced him from his Lord. In character, in ministry and in suffering he is united to him. That unity with Christ is the calling of every Christian believer. It is what baptism signifies (Romans 6:1–4) and it is our goal and ideal. Stephen seems to have reached it.

Thank God for his radical messengers. Listen to them. Do not ignore them because they are disturbing. They may be closer to Jesus than most of us!

The final word must go to those who stand in Stephen's shoes. If you are what used to be called one of the 'angry young men' or women of the church you may well be playing a vital role on behalf of your Lord in stirring up the church to be more faithful to him. But remember two things. For all the uncompromising nature of what Stephen said and did, he still did it with love and respect. Do not use your radical mission as an excuse for rudeness. You are not exempt from culti-vating the fruit of the Spirit in your life – and every aspect of it, at that (Galatians 5:22–23). Stephen clearly had it. That is what gave him the right to be so radical.

Secondly, if you want a radical ministry, be prepared to be treated as Stephen was. It will be uncomfortable for you as well as your audience. For Stephen it meant death. For you it might mean rejection in any number of other ways. But then, you did want to be truly identified with Jesus, didn't you? So, be prepared for the cost that is involved. Are you still so keen? Then, go for it!

Take it from here . . .

- Jesus was at the centre of Stephen's life; that is why his message was so powerful. What things in your life might be getting in the way, preventing you from having a powerful message to share about Jesus?

- Read Galatians 5:22–23. Like Stephen we need to show the fruits of the Spirit in *our* lives if we are to convince people with a disturbing message from God. What areas of your life need more transformation by the Holy Spirit? Ask him to help you.

- Have you ever heard other Christians criticising something about the church? How did you feel listening to them? Now that you have read this chapter about Stephen do you think your reaction was a right one? How can you react constructively to radical messages about the state of the church?

17

Philip

Working on the frontiers

Only one man in the New Testament bears the honoured title of 'evangelist' and that is Philip (Acts 21:8). Evangelism permeated every aspect of the life of the early church but it is surprising how little they analysed it and reflected on it. And the word evangelist itself only occurs a few times in the New Testament. Their emphasis was on *doing* evangelism rather than talking about it. We have reversed that emphasis with the result that our churches are in decline. Where you do find a growing church you find that someone is engaged in evangelism. If we want to learn more about evangelism from the Bible, we have to study the people who did it. And Philip is a prime example.

We first come across Philip when the apostles were proposing to appoint seven men to lead the Greek-speaking section of the church. Stephen was the outright leader but next in line was Philip. These men were chosen because they were 'known to be full of the Spirit and wisdom' (Acts 6:3). Philip was an impressive man whose qualities for spiritual leadership were obvious. It seems that when Stephen was martyred Philip stepped into his shoes and became the key leader among the Greek-speaking members of the church. That is probably why, when Stephen is removed from the scene, Luke turns his attention to the activities of this irrepressible evangelist.

Persecution came and all the church, except the apostles, moved out of Jerusalem. Philip found himself in Samaria and it is there that the story gets underway.

Taking the initiative

Finding himself in a new situation Philip seized the initiative and immediately began preaching the gospel (Acts 8:5). He did not wait for people to come to him, nor say that it was impossible for him to carry on because there was not any Christian fellowship there. He reminds me of Wesley's words to one of his converts. 'Sir,' he said, 'when you are a Christian you must either find fellowship or make it.' In the absence of other believers in Jesus, Philip chose to make it.

I wonder if he ever questioned whether he was doing the right thing. Until his mission there were no Samaritan converts, and Jews and Samaritans had not been on speaking terms for centuries.

Perhaps there were not meant to be Samaritan members of the church. Perhaps it was supposed to remain a purely Jewish movement. On the other hand, perhaps Philip recalled the words of the ascending Lord and remembered that the disciples were commissioned to be witnesses 'in Jerusalem, in all Judea and Samaria . . .' (Acts 1:8). Whatever his reservations might have been, he got down to the job.

An evangelist is one who seizes the initiative. He or she does not wait for opportunities to be created. He or she creates them. Two shoe salesmen were once sent to an island to establish a market for their company. One cabled home saying the journey had been a waste of money and effort. 'No one,' he said, 'wears shoes here.' The other cabled home enthusiastically, 'No one,' he said, 'wears shoes here, yet.' The second one had the character of an evangelist!

Inevitably, that means the evangelist has the job of working on the frontiers. Others are called to work within the church or on its fringes where they are usually met with some degree of encouragement and warmth. The evangelist is out in the cold, surrounded by unbelievers, often in a minority of one. Foolishly, the church often seems to misunderstand his role. Many evangelists are criticised for not entertaining the saints or for not being sufficiently in the orbit of the church. But is that where they are meant to be? Their place should rather be the pubs and clubs, the secular meeting places, the market stalls, the conferences and union meetings which are anything but Christian. We show our failure to understand by our failure to support evangelists – either financially or personally. It is a failure for which we are criminally responsible. The vast majority of people, even in Britain, will never hear the gospel if it is kept confined within the structures of the church. Evangelists *need* to work outside them.

The task must be a lonely one. For Philip that loneliness was accentuated not only by his move from Jerusalem to Samaria but by the next move he was called to make – from a successful and busy campaign in Samaria to meet just one man on a desert road. You cannot get much more isolated than that!

If you are contemplating taking up the work of an evangelist you must count the cost of being on the lonely frontier before you do so. If it is not your calling maybe you should consider 'adopting' an evangelist so that he or she can benefit from close personal support from a fellow believer.

Living under God's authority

Luke also tells us about Philip's authority for his work. His task was not just a matter of speaking words but of doing acts of power. In Samaria it was when the crowds heard his words 'and saw the miraculous signs he did [that] they all paid close attention to what he said' (Acts 8:6). Two special forms of miracle are named. Evil spirits were exorcised and disabled people were healed. The miracles recorded in the New Testament nearly always accompany the preaching of the good news as signs of its truth and power. The proclamation of the gospel is both verbal and visual. And it is the visual that lends credence to the verbal.

We have tried to duck this issue in many ways. We say miracles belonged to a former age but do not fit in our scientific and more secular atmosphere. There is no evidence to substantiate that conclusion, but plenty to question it – miracles do take place and there is a resurgence of interest in the supernatural. We can say that miracles belong only to the enthusiasts or the charismatics, but whatever excuse we like to make we cannot escape the clear picture given in the New Testament that evangelism involves both words and wonders.

Luke is concerned to demonstrate the authority of Philip's work in other ways too. Although his preaching was accompanied by miracles, Philip was not indifferent to the feelings of the senior church leaders in Jerusalem about his work in Samaria. They were soon invited down (Acts 8:14–17) to validate his work as being from God.

This step was vital if the centuries-old rift between Jew and Samaritan was to be healed within the church. In the process God graciously confirmed that the gospel was for the Samaritans too. This he did by sending his Holy Spirit on them as unmistakably as he had on the original disciples at Pentecost. Anything less than this would have for ever left a question mark in the Jewish church as to the legitimacy of the Samaritan converts. Even if they were accepted, they might have been seen as 'second class' members of the church. But now there could be no mistake. God's intention was clear.

The role of the apostles is interesting. We are sometimes too quick to drive a wedge between the work of the Spirit and the recognition of the church leaders. I know that some church leaders have asked for it! But Philip did not fall into this trap even though some of the people in Jerusalem must have had grave doubts about the rightness of Philip's work. However much an evangelist works on the frontiers, and however much his ministry is authenticated by the Spirit, he still needs to work in fellowship with the church. He dare not become an independent agent, answerable to no one therefore without responsibility to the wider church. Much damage has been caused by such arrogance and not a few evangelistic movements which have begun well have subsequently gone off the rails because they were not sufficiently related to the church.

In yet one more way Luke is concerned to show the authority for Philip's work. Three times we are told that Philip received his instructions from the Spirit. Such references suggest that Philip was finely tuned, spiritually. But they also tell us that evangelism which has not been initiated by the Spirit is really quite worthless. It is no different from what Jesus said about his own ministry in John 5:19: 'The Son can do nothing by himself; he can do only what he sees his Father doing, because whatever the Father does the Son also does.'

Our evangelism often lacks that fine tuning. We engage in it because we feel we must do something and we think we are being spiritual if we engage in busy activity. But unless we go to the people to whom the *Spirit* directs us we are wasting our time and wearing ourselves out in the process. In view of the immense need there is on every hand, too much need to respond to, we need to listen carefully to the Spirit's direction to know where our scarce resources are going to be used most for his glory. Many probably thought Philip was mad to desert the successful work of Samaria for a desert. But the Spirit knew what he was doing when he told Philip to go. Almost certainly a whole mission field was opened up through the conversion of that one man he met there. It is just as well he was listening to the Spirit's voice, rather than to people.

Philip's approach to his work

Philip's conversation with the man we have come to know simply as 'the Ethiopian eunuch' enables Luke to give us an insight into how Philip went about his work. In looking at the story we can pick up several important hints about evangelism.

First, Philip was concerned that the eunuch *understood* what he was reading (Acts 8:30). He was not concerned simply to get a 'decision' out of him. Converts who are emotionally blackmailed into making such decisions usually do not last. 'Easy come, easy go,' applies to converts as much as to anything else. There is a certain appeal in working for instant success but we must resist the temptation. The evangelical wing of the church has suffered from decisionism. The New Testament is more concerned about the experience of the converted life than the experience of conversion itself. Certainly we must preach and work for verdicts. But we must do so with respect for a person's emotional and intellectual integrity. The gospel calls for understanding.

Secondly, Philip was concerned to be *relevant*. Verse 35 tells us that 'Philip began with that very passage . . .', the one the eunuch was reading and puzzling over. Admittedly it was a gift for someone wishing to explain the gospel, since it was Isaiah 53. Even so, it reminds us that we must start with the questions, puzzles and arguments of the people whom we seek to win for Christ. Too often we have been embarrassed by them or unable to handle them and so have shifted ground. But evangelism that moves the goal posts is rarely effective.

Thirdly, Philip was concerned to speak of *Jesus*. We can summarise Philip's message in the words of verse 35; he 'told him the good news about Jesus'. It is staggering just how little Jesus figures in so-called evangelistic preaching these days. We often hear about the preacher and his converts, or even about the church and its failures. Sometimes, and this is certainly getting warmer, we hear some decent Pauline theology. But the heart of the matter is Jesus. The gospel preached by the apostles was totally bound up with Jesus, his life, death and resurrection. Paul tells us as much in 1 Corinthians 15:3–4.

We live in a generation that knows literally nothing of Jesus. Young people in our schools today do not know his name. They do note know he existed, what he did and taught or why he died and they certainly do not know that he rose again. But *he* is the good news we must tell them. Somehow we must learn to drop much of our baggage, get back to basics and talk of him.

Fourthly, we may note how *thorough* Philip was. As they travelled along, the eunuch asked Philip to baptise him. Presumably he did this because Philip had talked with him about baptism. If not they soon put the item on their agenda and got around to it. It is a reminder that we are not only to make converts but to disciple them by teaching them to observe Jesus' commandments (Matthew 28:20). We dare not short-change potential converts by failing to teach them thoroughly about Jesus. Superficial messages which fail to show the ethical implications of the gospel or do not mention the importance of entering a Christian fellowship will not produce mature Christians.

The problems Philip faced

In giving us a full portrait of Philip's work, Luke does not neglect the opposition he faced. In Samaria Philip's ministry was a cause of great joy (Acts 8:8). But with the joy there are always problems and Philip did not escape them. For him the problem came in the form of one of his supposed converts, Simon the Sorcerer, known as the Great Power. This man had had everything going for him – until Philip appeared on the scene with greater power. Simon the Sorcerer was overawed by the miracles he saw Philip do. The Bible tells us that he 'believed and was baptised' (Acts 8:13). But soon afterwards things went drastically wrong.

In conversation with Peter and John, who had arrived from Jerusalem, Simon began to show his real motives. He asked for the laying-on of hands so that the power he had seen in Philip and in them could be his. It seems as if he only 'believed' and was baptised in order to tap the source of the Spirit's power for his own ends.

It is a comfort to know that even so gifted an evangelist as Philip had failures among his converts and once, at least, baptised a convert who was distinctly suspect! It would be nice to be able to claim that every person who believed and was baptised was genuine and continued to grow in Christ from that moment on. But the reality is very different. We all have our disappointments and our failures. People often come to Christ from very mixed motives. Some, like Simon, seek to use Christianity for their own ends and when it does not give them what they want they go off in a huff.

We do not know the outcome. After Peter's stern rebuke, Simon asks for prayer but whether he demonstrated true repentance or was simply trying to avoid the consequences of his manipulation of spiritual power we do not know. But thank God for the Bible's honesty. Not everything that Philip did was one hundred per cent successful.

Philip's family

Luke gives us one further glimpse of Philip. Years later when Paul was on his way back to Jerusalem from Greece he and his party stayed with Philip in Caesarea (Acts 21:8). We get a lovely glimpse of Philip and his family from that visit. 'He had', we read, 'four unmarried daughters who had the gift of prophecy.' They were followers of Jesus and active in their use of the spiritual gifts they had received. Philip's preaching elsewhere had obviously not been at their expense. They had not grown up to hate Jesus because Dad was always away or busy with other people.

Responsibility to the family is one of the biggest issues facing any full-time worker for Christ and many voluntary workers for him too. We must affirm that Christian leaders have a responsibility to demonstrate the gospel first *within their own homes* and that their message to the world is contradicted if their own homes are in chaos. Of course children have a mind of their own and their waywardness is not always to be blamed on their parents! But Philip is certainly a model to imitate. His vigorous evangelism, which had often sent him to the isolated frontiers alone, had not been at the expense of the spiritual development of his own children.

This final glimpse of Philip is a fitting end to a very full portrait of this man from whom we can learn much about being a messenger of Christ. If we too seek the honoured title of 'evangelist' there is no one better to study than him.

Take it from here . . .

- Think of one or two full-time evangelists you know. In what practical ways can you support them and their families in their work?

- Philip was sensitive to the Spirit's leading. Take some time to pray about specific ways in which God might want to use you. Ask him to direct you today into work for him.

- Your family needs you, too! Think about it – are any members of your family missing out on your time and care because you are so busy with 'Christian' things? If so, spend some time now reviewing your timetable.

18

Paul

Keeping a foot in both camps

We all think of the apostle Paul as head and shoulders above virtually everyone else in church history. He is *the* pioneer missionary. He is *the* writer of the New Testament, even though others contributed a few works! He is *the* most influential person to have shaped the early church. Evangelist, missionary, pastor, theologian, administrator, intellectual with the common touch – he had it all.

But I doubt that he was seen in this light in his own day however much people recognised the contribution he made. Then he was one among several gifted leaders in the church and people were not afraid to argue with him, abandon him or criticise him. He has much more in common with us than we perhaps realise.

The man

It is true that Saul of Tarsus was equipped for his task as missionary to the Gentiles by a unique combination of gifts and background experiences. He was born in the city of Tarsus and, from what he said when arrested in Jerusalem, he was proud of it (Acts 21:39). It was the principal city of the fertile plain of East Cilicia and was prosperous. It was also a place devoted to the pursuit of culture, philosophy and learning. It was a 'university city' second to none, even though Athens was better known. So it is not surprising that Paul shows himself to be thoroughly at home in a Greek environment and to have made full use of the training he would have received in rhetoric and debate.

He was also glad to say that he was a Roman citizen. Acts 22:28 tells us that he inherited the status from his father. How he acquired the privilege in spite of being a Jew we cannot tell. But Paul was not averse to making use of the rights that citizenship conferred on him. It meant that, anywhere in the Roman Empire, he was entitled to a fair public trial, to exemption from certain degrading punishments and to protection from summary execution. When he appealed to Caesar for a fair trial (Acts 25:10) he was making use of his ultimate privilege as a Roman citizen. It is easy to see how much his mission benefitted from the protection and privileges accorded by this status.

All that would have been quite useless unless he had also been thoroughly Jewish. He was after all going to be the messenger of a Jewish Messiah and to work in co-operation with an infant Jewish church. Here too his pedigree was impeccable. Born in Tarsus and educated in a Greek environment it might have been expected to be less than pure. Despite birth into the tribe of Benjamin it could have been that, given his upbringing, he was a Hellenist, a Greek-speaking Jew. But not so! He was a 'Hebrew of Hebrews' (Philippians 3:5), that is, a Hebrew-speaking Jew and so he could boast a linguistic and a cultural purity. Furthermore, he was a Pharisee. He belonged to the strictest party of the Jews who observed the law more conscientiously and treated it more seriously than any other people of his day. His Jewish credentials could pass the most minute scrutiny.

So, in this one man, God brought the three ancient worlds of Rome, Greece and Israel together and through his upbringing uniquely prepared him to bridge the cultural divides with the message of the gospel.

Some Christians find it easy to write off culture, learning or the advantages of a certain background. Paul does not do so. When he refers to it as 'rubbish' and writes it off as a loss (Philippians 3:7, 8) we must be careful to understand what he is claiming. None of this, he says, is of the slightest advantage when it comes to *salvation*. It will not get him to heaven on a motorway whilst others have to struggle with the journey on a 'B' road. There is only one road to heaven but many ways of preaching the gospel. Paul was prepared to use every means and exploit every advantage to do that.

It is not only Paul to whom God has given a particular background which he can use. Each of us has a unique background. Whether it lies in a cultured university city or a dockyards inner city, the Civil Service or the dole queue, God has given us an ability to speak to a certain group of people in a language they will understand and which others will not. So, at one end of the scale, people like Cliff Richard in the entertainment world are not necessarily called to turn their backs on that world when they become Christians. God has given them gifts and placed them in a network of contacts to be exploited for him. At the other end of the spectrum people like Mark, a friend of mine who works in the docks doing jobs that I could never do in a thousand years, are equally able to be messengers for God. Being accepted socially does not, of course, mean that the message we bring will be accepted. God not only gave Paul a background and an intellect, but a body and a personality. Again we can see how God had prepared these, even his weaknesses, and ordained that they too should be used productively for the gospel.

Tradition, probably accurately, tells us Paul was a sturdy little man with bow-legs and a prominent nose! He himself implies that he was nothing much to look at. The lack of striking appearance was a deliberate strategy on God's part to make sure people would pay attention to the message and not spend their time looking at the messenger, as Paul well understood (2 Corinthians 4:4, 7).

That Paul was tough is self-evident. To have gone through the hardships, beatings, imprisonments and shipwrecks, in addition to all that unenviable travelling he did, and still to have survived, must have meant he was tough. But he was not physically perfect and some illness or defect, to which he alludes in 2 Corinthians 12:7 and again in Galatians 4:13–15, was a constant reminder that he was only human. Whatever the disability was, he desperately longed to be free. But that was one prayer that God never answered with a 'Yes'.

The most famous example of how God still works in this way is, I suppose, Joni Eareckson Tada. Paralysed in a diving accident, Joni is now confined to a wheelchair. In the early days after the accident she questioned God constantly about her suffering and longed for healing. But she has been far more effective for Christ from her wheelchair, through writing, singing and art, than she would probably ever have been otherwise. I think, too, of the joy of a friend of mine recently after he had just visited an elderly member of his church in hospital. He could not believe the effect she was having in that hospital ward as a messenger for Jesus.

As to personality, Paul was a passionate man. We see him in various moods – fretful, anxious, impatient. He could be fiery and quick-tempered, as his argument with Peter shows (see Galatians 2). But he could also be very warm-hearted and sensitive as his letters to the

Corinthian church equally demonstrate. His passionate personality, harnessed to Christ, gave him the fire to be a pioneer with the gospel, going where no one had gone before. Others were content to stay on more familiar territory. He kept forging ahead, restlessly claiming more and more territory for Christ. His commitment sometimes led to misunderstandings, as when he and Barnabas fell out over the treatement of John Mark (Acts 15:36–40). He probably never suffered fools gladly! But without that passion he would never have been the pioneer he was.

We need to recognise that the work of evangelism still calls for passionate people to do it – that is what makes some evangelists superb preachers but difficult team members. It also explains why many find it difficult to work with a cautious church. Our ideas of holiness usually mean that we think people should not be fiery or impatient and it would be wrong to pretend that such characteristics are not likely to lead us into sin. The person who can preach most persuasively may also be liable to use his tongue most destructively. The person who has an unflappable trust in God can also be so laid back that he or she is negligent of people's needs. So it was with Paul. The passion which fired him for the gospel could – and on occasions did – distance him from his fellow believers.

But God is able to use even our weaknesses for his glory. Often the very weaknesses others see in our personalities are precisely the strengths God uses to establish some particular work for him. Paul might well have been difficult to live with but God knew what he was doing by calling him and exploited his restlessness to make him a pioneer. This does not justify sin but it should make us look at ourselves and others and ask how God can turn the weaknesses we see into his strengths.

The motive

I suspect that Paul would have been a leader among men whatever he had turned his hand to. He was that sort of person. But one thing decisively turned him to Christ and provided him with a clear and constant motivation for his missionary work. That was his conversion experience on the Damascus Road.

He never tired of telling his story and he frequently used his encounter with the risen Christ as the basis for his defence or as a framework for preaching the gospel. Acts records a number of times when he blatantly did so (see Acts 22:1–22 and 26:1–31). But the story keeps coming through in his letters as well. In Philippians 3:1–11 he tells it in a more theological light. His meeting with the ascended Lord in blinding light is undoubtedly behind such statements as that in 2 Corinthians 4:6; 'For God, who said, "Let light shine out of darkness," made his light shine in our hearts to give us the light of the knowledge of the glory of God in the face of Christ.'

It becomes evident that it is his own personal experience which coloured all his preaching when, towards the end of his life, he writes to his young protégé, Timothy. He speaks of the way Christ came to save sinners and claims to have been the worst of them. Then he says, 'But for that very reason I was shown mercy so that in me, the worst of sinners, Christ Jesus might display his unlimited patience as an example for those who would believe on him and receive eternal life' (1 Timothy 1:16). Then he bursts into a song of praise.

Paul's conversion was meant to be a showcase in which the power of the gospel was displayed. If God could forgive and change him, murderous prig that he was; if God could get through to his hard heart, trained and argumentative Pharisee that he was; if God could change his mind, disinclined to repent though he was, he could do it to anyone! There was no room for despair about the apparent weakness of the gospel message. There was every room to say, as Paul did in the face of all the impressive pomp and power of Rome, 'I am not ashamed of the gospel, because for it is the power of God for the salvation of everyone who believes, first for the Jew, then for the Gentile' (Romans 1:16).

It was his own experience which drove him on in preaching the gospel. Having encountered the grace of God as he did, he had no option: 'Woe to me,' he said, 'if I do not preach the gospel!'

The greatest evangelists are still those in whom God has brought about a dramatic change in life. You do not have to tell them to witness! They do so naturally. Putting them on a personal evangelism course may even spoil them. They just blurt out the good news in all sorts of circumstances when 'more experienced' Christians would often be more refined. It is because we do not really know what God has done for us that we find we do not know what to say about him. The place to begin, if you really want to be a messenger of God, is in your own encounter with the risen Christ. Paul never lost the wonder of it. And, if it is real, you will not either. Can you recount a conversion experience or some form of renewal experience when you sensed Christ in a special way? If not, why not set aside some time and devote yourself, perhaps with some friends, to seeking God in a fresh way and finding a new anointing of the Holy Spirit?

The method

Paul was so consumed by the need to preach the gospel that he was ready to use any method which was consistent with the gospel itself in order to do so. He defends this approach in writing to the Corinthians. The publication of the gospel is so important that he says, 'I have become all things to all men so that by all possible means I might save some' (1 Corinthians 9:22).

We ought perhaps to explore the qualification Paul built into that statement elsewhere before seeing how it works out in practice. It becomes clear that there are limits to the variety of means he would use because some means would actually be inconsistent with the gospel itself. The gospel is a message of integrity. The messenger must not therefore be lacking in integrity as he preaches it. Writing again to the Corinthians Paul explains that he has rejected 'secret and shameful ways': making unrealistic promises or changing the message in any way. 'On the contrary, by setting forth the truth plainly we commend ourselves to every man's conscience in the sight of God' (2 Corinthians 4:2).

The medium must be consistent with the message. That rules out certain techniques of evangelism such as subliminal advertising, or door-to-door salesmanship which keeps the small print hidden until the dotted line has been signed. It further rules out the use of certain cultural media which obscure rather than highlight the gospel. Certain forms of music may be inappropriate, for example. Terminology which implies that the gospel is no more than a drug trip or a variation of certain kinds of philosophy, such as existentialism which leaves little place for the objective facts of the gospel, may equally be inappropriate.

Having said that, the field is wide open. Paul himself leads the way. The message may not change but the cultural package in which it is delivered is adapted so that the hearers can make sense of it. In the synagogue Paul could argue about the promised Messiah and the meaning of the Old Testament, using the structure of the synagogue service to do so. In a Gentile market-place, however, the synagogue message would have been meaningless. So Paul translates the truth about Jesus, presenting him as 'Lord' rather than 'Messiah', which made more sense in the Roman Empire. Paul is able, too, to latch on to features in the cultures of those to whom he spoke, such as the poets and philosophers he quotes at Athens (Acts 17:16–33), to lead them to the truth.

On the mission field today the whole question of the cultural package in which the message has been delivered is being taken much more seriously than before. Too often in the past, the Christian gospel has been identified with a Western materialist life-style and Western political ideas. In the United Kingdom, too, the Christian message has become identified with certain cultural forms, which are not inherent to it at all. It has been identified with middle-class forms of dress, for instance, or with a love of organs, or with certain programmes within the church which have long since lost any Christian content, or just with good works and charity collections. Paul challenges us to a much greater liberty in our preaching of the gospel. We must break out from our cultural ghetto if we are to be true to the original evangelists. Different forms of service, times of meeting, forms of music, places to operate and ways of saying things, may well mean we become more effective messengers of God and would not involve any inconsist-ency with the gospel we want to preach.

On a more practical level still, we might comment on the actual methods Paul used. He frequently gives his testimony. He is also keen on debating and much of the time, when in a Jewish synagogue and elsewhere, he was not so much preaching, as arguing. He does not make statements for people to take or leave but really tries to convince them that he is right. He does so by demolishing their objections and persuasively setting out his side of the argument. The Good News Bible translation of Acts 19:8 puts it well, 'Paul went into the synagogue and during three months spoke boldly with the people, holding discussions with them and trying to convince them about the Kingdom of God.' The persuasive discussion approach seemed a fairly common method. So today, debate within a university or dialogue with those of other religions may well be the most appropriate method of evangelism providing we start from the conviction that Jesus alone is the way.

He also preached and taught, as we would understand those things today. At Ephesus, after the three-month period just mentioned, he hired a hall and taught a full three-year course in Christianity. Often he was forced to engage in much more hit-and-run evangelism. But he never did this because he wanted to, only because circumstances compelled him to. Where he had the chance of church planting over a longer term, he took it.

He also made effective use of letter writing. Romans and Galatians are marvellous expositions of the gospel and have served down the centuries as excellent evangelistic tracts as well as being pastoral letters to the churches. It would be intriguing to know how many more letters he wrote which are not recorded in the New Testament. But the Holy Spirit knows best and has left us only these! We see only the tip of the iceberg. Writing letters remains a key method of evangelism – one in which the house-bound and otherwise inactive people are supremely important. Evangelism is not restricted to those who are able to get about. Paul did some of his most effective work in a prison cell, chained to a Roman soldier! I think of a house-bound woman in our city who has led a stream of visitors to Christ, and of others who are very restricted but who invite their neighbours round or write letters to pen pals. Limited circumstances do not rule us out from being God's messengers.

The final method Paul used was to send envoys. Even Paul could not be in two places at once. We know he made good use of people like Titus and Timothy to act as his messengers. This is not an excuse for doing evangelism by proxy and then feeling we have discharged our duty! But there is room not only to engage in evangelism oneself but to train and support others in doing it, especially when our own movements are restricted.

The message

'We do not preach ourselves, but Jesus Christ as Lord . . .' (2 Corinthians 4:5).

The message Paul preached was Jesus. There was no other message at all. Several implications follow.

Paul did not preach himself. Some so-called messengers of God are so full of their own ministries, as Paul's opponents were at Corinth, that Jesus hardly gets a mention.

Paul preached a 'full' Christ. His understanding of Christ was rich and exhaustive. He did not stick with one superficial explanation of Jesus as we sometimes hear today, like, 'Jesus wants to be your friend.' The unpopular bits were there: Jesus was crucified. The incredible bits were there: he rose from the dead. The difficult bits were there: Jesus was the one through whom and for whom the world was made. The theological bits were there: the fullness of the Godhead was in Jesus.

Paul never departed from this message. Jesus is not the basic gospel from which, after conversion, you graduate to something else. The message is for the unbeliever and the mature Christian. The invitation is always to take a fuller look at Jesus in order to find in him not only the basic message of repentance and forgiveness, but the answer to questions of relationships within the church, to questions of spiritual experience or of ethical debate and anything else you need. Paul's pastoral work within the churches was simply a continuation of his evangelistic work in the world. All he ever did was to preach Christ fully as the occasion demanded.

If we were as Christ-centred in our preaching today we might be as effective as the apostle Paul. Our trouble is that we often do not have Paul's confidence either in Christ or in the power of his gospel.

Take it from here . . .

- Paul based much of his preaching on his own experience of God. Imagine you are talking to a neighbour. What could you share about God from your personal experience?

- God used everything Paul had, including weaknesses! Think about your background and personality – is there anything God could exploit if you let him? Ask the Holy Spirit to show you.

- Check your culture! Have you got any expectations of the way Christians should behave that are cultural rather than biblical? How can you tell which are which?

19

Apollos

Using what you are

We can be very choosy about the type of preachers we follow. The trend today is to go for the preacher who is a great story-teller and entertainer. Preachers who are solid and intellectual do not attract a great crowd. The church, I am often told, is dying 'by degrees'.

The truth is that God has a place for messengers of good news from a whole variety of backgrounds. Some, like the famous evangelist D L Moody, may be unable to speak the Queen's English properly, whilst others, like C T Studd, may come out of the top drawer of society. The variety of people God uses may be one of the most powerful illustrations of the gospel itself – a gospel which breaks down the dividing walls which people build on racial, cultural or social lines (Ephesians 2:14–18).

Recently, three of my fellow ministers and I took part in an evangelistic dinner. We were *not* invited to preach, and the invitation made that very clear, but to give a personal word of testimony. We were limited to twelve minutes each! It was both an interesting and effective evening.

First to speak was a Yorkshire Methodist who knew all the fullness of the Methodist experience of conversion, thanks to a godly Sunday School teacher, and had experienced a touch of renewal long after he had entered the ministry. Next came the Pentecostal pastor who had grown up in downtown Belfast and was 'frightened' into the kingdom of God through a brush, albeit minor, with the police as a teenager. I followed, the Grammar School boy from a southern sea-side Christian home. My childhood commitment to Christ had been reinforced after an intellectual examination of the evidence for believing whilst studying sociology at a Northern University. Finally came the vicar of our civic church. He had been brought up in the home counties, been through public school, the army and Oxford university and had been converted through a CSSM evangelist. Different, but God uses us all in our diversity.

If you think that God can use most people but have doubts about those with a cultured intellectual background, maybe Apollos can help.

We do not know how Apollos became a Christian. It may well have been in his native Alexandria where Christianity had gained a foothold early on. But we know that God used all the blend of his cultured background and natural gifts, transformed by the Spirit, to make him a first-rate evangelist and a 'great help to those who by grace had believed' (Acts 18:27).

Alexandria, a city in North Africa, was one of the most famous cultural centres of the ancient world. Growing up there Apollos would have had the benefit of the famous synagogue, of a fine Greek education with its emphasis on oratory, and of the city's impressive library. It was there that the Greek version of the Old Testament, known as the Septuagint, was produced. Apollos would have imbibed that intellectually stimulating atmosphere from his earliest days.

So it should come as no surprise when we read that he was a 'learned' or 'eloquent' man (Acts 18:24). Probably both these words allude to the same thing. He was cultured. He appears to have been the ancient version of an Oxbridge graduate – the best that civilisation could produce, so some would tell us.

His outstanding characteristics

When we first meet him in the Bible we find him at Ephesus. It is there that four outstanding characteristics – ideals for any messenger of God – become apparent.

First, he knew what he was talking about. He had a thorough grasp of the Scriptures and 'had been instructed in the way of the Lord'. Such a knowledge would have been acquired painfully, through hours of study and years of learning. He had obviously been prepared to listen to others and learn from them. He did not believe that the Holy Spirit made such study unnecessary. Spiritual gifts did not make his mind redundant. That study proved invaluable again and again as he 'vigorously refuted the Jews in public debate, proving from the Scriptures that Jesus was the Christ' (Acts 18:28).

In our 'instant' age Christian people tend to be impatient with study. If it can be taught in a ten-minute sermon or read in a full-colour visual presentation in a couple of minutes, or remembered as a simple slogan – fine. If not, we will not bother with it. 'Why bother training at Bible College? The task is urgent! Let's get on with it!' But often such an approach leads to disaster as evangelists and pastors find they have not got the depth to sustain their ministry or the answers to refute their critics.

Secondly, Apollos was enthusiastic. He spoke 'with great fervour.' It may be that this does not so much refer to natural exuberance as to Spirit-given passion. Either way, he escaped the pitfall common to many academics: being a bore. The knowledge he had was not knowledge he held in an uncommitted sort of way. He was not apathetic about it. It had *moved* him and, being convinced that others needed to share in the good news that he had discovered, he bent all his abilities and arguments to persuade them of the truth.

Thirdly, he was teachable. Apollos is something of a puzzle. On the one hand we read that he 'taught about Jesus accurately' but on the other hand 'he knew only the baptism of John' (Acts 18:25). This probably means that there was nothing wrong with what he said but that there were a few gaps in his knowledge.

The lovely thing is that when Priscilla and Aquila (see next chapter) approached him about the matter, which they did with great discretion and sensitivity, he responded with great humility. Gifted as he was, and used by God though he was, he did not assume that he was infallible or knew it all. He obviously believed not only in thorough preparation before he spoke to others about the Lord but in on-the-job training as he did so. Maybe that is a lesson for some of us who fall into the trap, not of doing too little training but too much, with the result that we never actually start the job!

We should also note that he seems to have been taught further essentially by a woman, Priscilla. Many might have rejected that further teaching purely on the basis that a woman was giving it! But it did not seem to worry Apollos. He showed much greater openness than some contemporary Christian leaders to the vital part women can play in the church.

Fourthly, he was a gifted man. As an evangelist he

was a first-rate apologist, that is, he could set out the arguments for faith in Jesus and show people why other religious options are inadequate. He 'vigorously refuted the Jews in public debate, proving from the Scriptures that Jesus was the Christ' (Acts 18:28). Obviously he did not allow his vigour to run away with him, mentally arm-twisting people into the kingdom. When Paul preached in a number of places he provoked opposition but we never read of Apollos doing so. He must have been of a more gentle disposition and more winsome personality.

It is often said that you cannot argue people into the kingdom. In one sense that is absolutely true. Faith comes through a revelation of the spirit (2 Corinthians 4:1–6). And yet Apollos is being perfectly consistent with the whole thrust of evangelism as presented in Acts by using every argument he can muster to convince people that Jesus is Lord. Acts, as we have already seen, often uses the word 'persuade' (see Acts 17:4, 18:4, 19:8) to describe the evangelistic methods of the early preachers. They did not preach in the sense we usually mean, proclamatory monologue, but they used debates, conversations, lectures and a host of other techniques in order to convince people of the truth.

His different style

Apollos's gifts did not lead him to work on the frontiers. He was primarily a good teacher for those who already believed, gifted at helping them to understand the faith, as well as being a good apologist on their behalf. If he served as an evangelist it was usually on territory already opened up by someone else.

He was obviously a popular preacher. There was

standing room only when he was at the synagogue or church. Perhaps he was a bit less direct than Paul and perhaps a bit less obscure than Peter, tied up as he was with Jewish laws. His sermons would probably have made brilliant essays, polished, poetic, thoughtful and deep, bordering on the philosophical. And many people would have been convinced by that sort of thing. It appealed.

The lovely thing is that there is no sense of rivalry between Paul and Apollos. The way in which Paul constantly plays himself off against Apollos in 1 Corinthians 1–4 makes it plain that Paul trusted Apollos and that there was no jealousy between them. There is no hint of Paul resenting Apollos's different style and he never tried to do him down. In fact Paul trusted Apollos so much that he wanted him to visit Corinth once more on his behalf (1 Corinthians 16:12). There was room for both personalities and both approaches. Indeed Paul recognised that they were simply partners, with others, in a process initiated and empowered by God. Paul did stage one – he planted the churches – Apollos was particularly adept at stage two – he watered them. But God made the churches grow (1 Corinthians 3:6).

The world of big Christian events seems to be dominated by 'personalities'. Some of our big conferences and media techniques promote them. And naturally, because of our own intellectual and social backgrounds we may well prefer one preacher to another. But such choices are both unnecessary and wrong. They are unnecessary because all of them are our brothers and sisters in Christ, given to the church by God. 'All things are yours, whether Paul or Apollos or Cephas . . . and you are of Christ and Christ is of God' (1 Corinthians 3:21–22). They are wrong because to extol one preacher over another is to link your Christian identity with them rather than with the God about whom they speak.

We sometimes need a greater breadth in our vision of who are the real messengers of God. God uses people of all backgrounds and social classes; the clever, cultured and well-heeled as much as the more average and less educated. We do not have to choose between them but can welcome them all as his messengers.

Take it from here . . .

- Apollos learned to evangelise 'on the job'. How can you train yourself 'on the job'? Perhaps you could get a friend to listen to the way you talk about your faith and to comment on anything they think a non-Christian might find misleading or difficult to understand. Make some definite plans now.

- Is there a leader in your church from whom you do not find it easy to learn? What is it that makes it difficult for you to do so? If it is a fault in him or her try to set that aside in your mind to look more clearly at what he or she *can* teach you. If you feel the fault lies with you, what practical steps can you take – perhaps with the help of your housegroup or a Christian friend – to learn from his or her teaching or example?

- If there was a mission at your church, who would you want to come to lead it? Why? Be honest – are you in danger of falling into the trap of personality cults? What guidelines would you draw up in order to decide who to invite to lead such a mission?

20

Priscilla and Aquila
Seizing the opportunity

Paul's missionary work would have been quite impossible except for a number of people who provided hospitality and support in many ways. Among the people
who did so, and whom he valued very highly as fellow-
workers (Romans 16:3) were Priscilla and Aquila. They
were rare in many ways but not least because they are
the only married couple to be mentioned in the New
Testament as serving Christ in a joint ministry. Doubt-
less there were many others. But in all other cases only
one partner gets mentioned. The other is very much in
the background. Here was a couple where both had
much to give.

Paul had a natural affinity with them because they
earned their living as he did, by making tents. He first
came across them in Corinth where he probably spotted
their business and asked if they had room for another
worker. Wandering preachers, not all of whom were
Christians, often used to earn their living by plying their
trade wherever they went. But the relationship with
Priscilla and Aquila quickly went much further as they
too were Christians. Paul soon moved in over the shop
and they formed a deep and lasting friendship with him.
But that is to anticipate the story.

Partnership

Acts 18 gives us quite a lot of factual information about them. Aquila, the husband, was a Jew who came from Pontus on the Black Sea. He had moved to Rome where it seems that he and his wife Priscilla became founder members of the Christian church. Certainly they were Christians before they left Rome. They left Rome because in AD 49 or 50 the Emperor Claudius issued an edict which expelled all the Jews from the city. Suetonius, the Roman historian, tells us that the edict was the result of the Jews rioting 'at the instigation of Chrestus'. So Priscilla and Aquila made their way east to Corinth where they set up in business, once more, as tent-makers.

What of Priscilla? It is more difficult to come by hard factual information about her but there is no serious reason to doubt the common suggestions which are offered. Her name Priscilla, or as she is sometimes called more formally Prisca, suggests that she was not a Jew. But her marriage to Aquila probably indicates that she was a 'god-fearer' or inquirer after truth and a follower of the Jewish religion even before her conversion to Christ.

What arouses curiosity most about these two is that in five out of the seven references to them in the New Testament Priscilla is mentioned first. It may mean nothing more than that she was the most gifted one in Christian work and so her name tended, in Christian circles, to trip off the tongue first. Whether rightly or wrongly it is often the case that wives take a more public role in Christian service.

There is another explanation as to why Priscilla is usually mentioned first which may equally well be true.

It is suggested that she came from a higher social class than Aquila or was the partner in the marriage with financial security. Though that would have been unusual in that culture they still managed to work as the perfect partnership.

Christian couples can provide powerful illustrations of the gospel through their relationships with each other, especially in these days when marriage breakdowns are all too common. But Priscilla and Aquila illustrate the wider value of partnership in their support of Paul. They had a ministry in their own right but they were equally willing to support the ministry of Paul.

God often chooses to use us in partnership with others. Pastors, missionaries and evangelists on the front line need committed praying people at home. Without such people keeping in touch, sending out their newsletters and giving financial support their work would be impossible.

The idea of partnership has recently expanded beyond links between individuals to include links between churches. Some churches engage in partnership missions overseas, sending teams of people both ways for mutual encouragement. Others have formed partnerships between larger and smaller churches, and between suburban and inner-city churches so that inspiration can flow both ways and faith might be shared and stimulated. The openness of Priscilla and Aquila is an encouragement to explore such options.

Mobility

Priscilla and Aquila adopted, whether by choice or necessity, what we often consider to be a peculiarly modern form of lifestyle. They were mobile. Perhaps they could not help moving from Rome in the first place and setting up home in Corinth. But they left Corinth with Paul to live in Ephesus (Acts 18:18) and subsequently we read of them back in Rome (Romans 16:3–4). The outstanding fact to notice about these two, however, is that wherever they went they immediately got stuck into Christian witness and joined with others in Christian fellowship.

Mobility is one of the most dangerous threats to Christian commitment today. When a family moves from one area to another they will often not join in a Christian church or get involved in new Christian service. Some people always have the intention of doing so but never quite get around to it. Others are more determined not to do so, having been over-committed in their previous church perhaps at the expense of their own family. They are determined not to make the same mistake again! So they fight shy of any attempt their new church makes to welcome them. Others have no real commitment to Christ in the first place, but rather a sentimental attachment to a particular building or group of people. So when they move they have no reason to perpetuate this social religion. Any attempt to encourage them to do so is likely to be met with a series of feeble excuses about the church being too far away, or the wrong denomination, or not like the old place.

I have been amazed in the course of my pastoral ministry at the number of Christians I have met who were once thoroughly committed to a church but then moved and all commitment ceased. If you are among the mobile, beware. Follow the example of Priscilla and Aquila and seize the opportunity, wherever you are, to serve Christ fully.

On the other hand, mobility can provide us with immense opportunities for Christ. It all depends on our attitude. The world is much more open now than it ever has been and clearly some Christians have got the vision of seizing that fact with both hands. Many couples show a healthy independence from their family and roots, being prepared to live wherever their professional skills will be employed while at the same time being a Christian witness and an encouragement to the indigenous church.

Such mobility is not without cost. What do you do about housing in this country? What about the children and their education? What about the language if you go abroad? And what about the distance from close relatives? We have a couple in our church confronting these questions at the moment. Long-term missionaries with Missionary Aviation Fellowship, they are shortly to return overseas to a new situation. The question is, where? If they go to some places where they are needed they will have to learn a new language and their children's education will be very different from their previous African and English education. But, as another missionary couple said to me, to be mobile for Jesus is a fantastic adventure! Why stay at home and live such predictable lives when the world is open in front of us? We can view mobility as a disturbing threat or as a welcome opportunity.

Hospitality

One thing seems to have made it easy for Priscilla and Aquila to welcome changes of scenery. They seem to have been very hospitable; they loved having people round to their house. As soon as Paul met up with them we read that he moved in with them (Acts 18:3)! When Apollos came to preach in Ephesus we read that immediately 'they invited him to their home' (Acts 18:26) and in the relaxed surroundings of their lounge they went to work on his defective theology! In 1 Corinthians 16:19 we read about the church that met in their house, perhaps indicating that they had a reasonable amount of wealth and were able to act as hosts to a few dozen people.

Hospitality is spoken of by Peter as a gift of the Spirit (1 Peter 4:9,10). For Priscilla and Aquila it opened the door to the exercise of many other spiritual gifts, such as the gift of teaching, which we often regard as more significant than hospitality. But if they had never used the gift of hospitality in the first place they may never have had the opportunity to teach, or to be involved in Paul's missionary endeavours. It is, as Jesus said, that 'whoever can be trusted with very little can also be trusted with much' (Luke 16:10).

If hospitality is a spiritual gift, it must be one of the most neglected charismatic gifts in the church today! My MAF missionary friends, as well as several Australian visitors, have recently remarked how closed the houses of English people seem to be to each other. The fortress mentality of the English – that every man's home is his castle – seems to have infected the church. People are protective about their property, their families and their leisure in an unhealthy way and so do not offer hospitality when they could.

The church in this country needs to recapture the vision of Priscilla and Aquila. To open your home to the single, the lonely, the bereaved and those whom others neglect may well be the most effective thing you can ever do as a messenger of Christ. Using your relaxed and comfortable rooms instead of the church's cold and official rooms may help to overcome many obstacles in people's minds at they ask about the gospel or meet

Christians for the first time. And in places where there is no church, such as on many council housing estates, it may be the *only* way to start building a Christian community.

Equally, offering hospitality to fellow Christians will enrich your own Christian life greatly. It needs to be done with a positive and joyful heart, and not as a burden and an obligation. Our own feelings about it will inevitably be conveyed to our children and they should grow up seeing the offering of hospitality as a delight; we want many more Priscillas and Aquilas in the church!

Partnership, mobility, hospitality. Priscilla and Aquila seized every opportunity given to them to further the work of Christ.

At one point we really do wish we knew more about this couple. Paul says of them that 'they risked their lives for me' and that all the churches of the Gentiles were grateful to them (Romans 16:4). How did they do that? When did they do that? Was it at Ephesus when Paul's preaching provoked a riot? Or was it on some other occasion, perhaps unknown and unrecorded? We cannot be sure.

We *can* be sure that they were not lacking in courage in their defence of the gospel. Danger did not make them hold back. They were prepared to sacrifice themselves for Christ.

When you meet people who have such a commitment to the gospel it cannot help but rebuke the weak-kneed, lily-livered, self-serving Christianity of the contemporary church in the West which goes for compromise all along the line. I once met a Christian leader in an Eastern bloc country whose family had suffered much for their Christian faith, as he himself had done. I asked him how the atheist state limited his witness and what restrictions he accepted. With a broad smile he replied, 'You must

159

remember this: you can do anything you like for the sake of the kingdom of God, there are no restrictions . . . providing you are prepared to pay the price!'

Priscilla and Aquila were obviously among those who were prepared to pay the price for being messengers of God. Are you?

Take it from here . . .

- Working in a partnership brings real strength. If you are married what can you and your partner do for God together? If you are single, what can you and a friend do for God by teaming up?

- Do you know any Christians who have just moved to your area? How can you welcome them into your home and church without making them feel threatened or 'got at'?

- Have you asked God for the gift of hospitality? Ask him to show you ways in which you can use your home and possessions for him.